AF687633

HER LIFE, HER MONEY

A WOMAN'S GUIDE
TO BUILDING WEALTH AND
FINANCIAL FREEDOM

CHRISTINA EWERE

Copyright 2026 by Christina Ewere
All rights reserved. Except for brief quotations in reviews, articles, or similar publications, no portion of this book may be reproduced, stored in a retrieval system, or transmitted in any form or by any means—electronic, mechanical, photocopy, recording, or other form—without prior written permission of the author or the publisher.

To my mother
Stella Irelamie
And my grandmothers
Elizabeth Olere
Christiana Oruebo

Contents

Introduction

"My mind on my money, my money on my mind"

-- **SNOOP DOGG**

My first job in Manhattan was an associate role at a large, Jewish family-owned insurance company. I had just completed my MBA in Texas and was determined to become the next Indra Nooyi.

But the journey was far from easy.

Surrounded by graduates from elite schools like Harvard University, the competition for finance jobs in New York City was fierce. To make matters more difficult, I was new to the city and had no close family or friends nearby to help ease the stress of building a career and finding my footing.

Like many children of immigrants, I was raised with a very specific definition of success. In our household, respectable careers fell into a narrow list: engineer, accountant, doctor, or lawyer. Stability mattered more than passion because stability meant survival. My mother believed accounting was especially smart for a woman: practical, respected, dependable, and unlikely to disappear during difficult economic times. My father, wanting the best for me, encouraged me to pursue a joint MBA-JD degree, a combination he believed would guarantee both prestige and financial security.

So, I followed the responsible path. While I didn't study accounting, I earned my Economics degree, completed my MBA, and entered the corporate world armed with spreadsheets, financial statements, and a carefully constructed plan for success.

But underneath all that practicality, I was deeply creative.

Even while in school, immersed in Finance and Economics theories, a part of me was always curious about art, storytelling, culture, fashion, media, and the endless possibilities of creative expression. I loved ideas, people, aesthetics, far more than balance sheets and financial models. The financial world never felt like a calling to me; it felt like security. A stable foundation to stand on while I figured out who I wanted to become.

Then I moved to New York City. Everywhere felt electric — full of ambition, creativity, and people reinventing themselves every day. During the day, I spent time working and learning the language of money and business. But outside the office, I found myself observing everything else: the confidence of women in media and fashion, the artists filling downtown cafés, the endless possibility that maybe life did not have to fit into the narrow categories I had grown up believing in.

Working in an insurance company only deepened that education. I started to understand that many successful people were not necessarily smarter or worked harder; they simply understood money differently. They knew how to protect assets, use credit strategically, invest early, and make decisions with a long-term mindset. Financial literacy gave them confidence in rooms where others felt intimidated. At the same time, I began to understand that financial knowledge is more than numbers on a spreadsheet. It is leverage, independence, and freedom. It teaches you how businesses operate, how wealth is built quietly over time, and how opportunity is often tied to understanding systems that many people are never taught to navigate.

So, while my peers may have focused on titles or status, I became fascinated by what was happening underneath the surface — cash flow, risk, debt, investment, negotiation, and long-term strategy.

Growing up, money conversations in immigrant households were often rooted in caution: save everything, avoid risk, work harder. But in the time I spent observing CEOs and executives, I began to see another side of financial knowledge, the ability to create opportunities instead of constantly living in fear of losing them. Some people inherited that confidence through family wealth and elite networks. Others had to build it from scratch.

What surprised me most was realizing that the analytical and creative parts of myself did not have to compete. Understanding finance gave me stability, but creativity gave me vision. New York was the first place that made me believe I might be able to build a life that included both.

What I began to understand during those years in the city was that financial knowledge for women is not just practical — it is deeply historical and personal.

For generations, women were not expected to navigate money on their own because they were not allowed to. Even when they worked, their labor was frequently undervalued or unpaid altogether. Housewives managed households, raised children, stretched family budgets, and often contributed invisible labor that kept entire families functioning, yet that work was rarely considered an economic contribution. Widows and divorced women often faced financial devastation because they had little legal or social protection. A woman could spend decades supporting a husband's career and still be left with no assets, no savings in her own name, and no guaranteed spousal support if the marriage ended.

Women who did pursue careers were often forced into a narrow set of "acceptable" professions — such as teaching, secretarial work or in my grandmother's case, nursing,— jobs considered extensions of caregiving rather than positions of authority or wealth-building. Even ambitious women were expected to prioritize marriage and motherhood above financial independence. Many were told directly that earning "too much" money or appearing too ambitious and independent would intimidate men and make them undesirable partners.

In parts of America, women were unable to open their own bank accounts without a male co-signer until the 1970s. Access to credit cards, mortgages, business loans, property ownership, and even basic financial autonomy were often tied to fathers or husbands. Society trained women to depend on men financially while simultaneously criticizing them for that dependence.

That history does not disappear overnight.

Even as opportunities expanded, many women still inherited unspoken messages about money: don't take risks, don't talk about finances, find security through marriage, prioritize stability over ambition. In immigrant households especially, those messages are often intensified because survival was always at stake. For many parents, encouraging daughters toward careers like accounting, medicine, law, or engineering was not about limiting dreams; it was about protection. Financial dependence was dangerous. Stability meant safety.

My mother understood that instinctively. She believed accounting would give me something no one could take away: the ability to support myself. At the time, I saw it as practical advice. Later, I realized it was also a form of generational wisdom passed down through women who understood how vulnerable life could become without financial independence.

Later in my career, upon entering the corporate finance world, I became increasingly aware of how differently men and women were taught to think about money. Men were often encouraged to invest, negotiate, take risks, and build wealth. Women were taught to save, sacrifice, and survive. Men discussed money openly as strategy and power; women were often expected to treat it quietly, almost apologetically. For example, for many years, salary transparency was discouraged in many workplaces.

As a result, women lacked the information needed to negotiate from a stronger position or benchmark their pay against peers in similar roles.

Financial literacy changes the way women move through the world.

Manhattan was expensive, and very quickly, survival began to outweigh idealism. Whatever creative dreams I quietly carried with me when I moved to New York had to take a backseat to practicality. Rent alone could humble you. Every paycheck already seemed to be spoken for before it arrived — subway fare, groceries, student loans, professional clothes, networking lunches, and the exhausting cost of simply trying to keep up in a city built on ambition.

That was another lesson many women, especially first-generation women, learned early: creativity often becomes a luxury when financial stability is uncertain.

So, practicality won, at least for the time being.

I focused on work, professional growth, and financial survival because I understood what was at stake. My family had sacrificed too much for me to treat stability casually. In a lot of immigrant families, financial success is never individual; it carries the weight of an entire family's hopes, fears, and sacrifices. Not only are you building a life for yourself, but you are also honoring the risks everyone took to get you there.

And as a woman, there was another layer to that pressure. Financial independence felt essential. I had seen too many women postpone their own ambitions because they lacked money of their own. Others stayed in unhealthy relationships, tolerated disrespectful workplaces, or abandoned creative passions because survival always came first.

So, while part of me was drawn toward creativity and self-expression, another part of me understood the quiet power of financial stability. Earning my own income, understanding investments, paying my own rent in Manhattan — those things may have seemed ordinary on the surface, but historically, for women, they represented something much larger: autonomy.

There were nights when I would come home exhausted from work, too drained to think and follow other creative pursuits, and I began to wonder whether adulthood simply meant becoming practical forever. But even then, the creative part of me never fully disappeared. It simply waited beneath the surface while I learned how to survive in a city that demanded resilience from everyone who wanted to remain.

In New York, I met women who appeared glamorous and successful on the surface but quietly relied entirely on partners or family wealth. I also met women who built financial independence from nothing and carried themselves with a completely different kind of confidence. The difference was not always income — it was knowledge. Knowing how money worked created freedom in ways that were almost invisible until you experienced it yourself.

It changes relationships because dependence becomes choice instead of necessity. It changes careers because women with financial confidence are more willing to negotiate salaries, invest in themselves, leave toxic work environments, or pursue creative ambitions without fear of failure. It changes identity because understanding how money works removes some of the fear that has historically kept women small.

It dawned on me. I could no longer just view finance from a cold or purely corporate lens. I began to see financial education as a form of empowerment, especially for women taught to prioritize security over self-determination. Understanding money was not just about greed and power. It was about having choices.

And for many women, having choices is still a relatively new form of freedom.

1

Compounding Interest and Opportunity Cost

"...invest, enterprise, take lucrative steps"

— **NIPSEY HUSSLE**

For many young women, it's easy to think that wealth is built through dramatic salary jumps. Getting promoted, earning six figures, starting a glamorous business, maybe even going viral on TikTok. Those may be great goals, but you will quickly understand that they will not guarantee you riches.

In the earliest days of my career, an older manager at a company I worked for noticed how ambitious I was, but he also noted my millennial impatience. It is a trait that exists in many millennials and perhaps Gen-Z alike, an urge to seek instant gratification, expect rapid career advancement, and seek constant mentorship, heightened by the prevalence of on-demand technology. The point was, I had been there less than a year and he could already see the dollar signs in my eyes amid my growing restlessness.

One day after a meeting, he called me into his office.

I expected feedback about my work.

Instead, he handed me about 30 pages of downloaded online articles from a well-known brokerage company and said "When you have some down time, I want you to read this carefully. Your greatest advantage right now isn't your salary or a promotion. It's your age."

I was confused.

At 25, a pretax income of $6,000 a month felt small compared to the lifestyle I wanted.

I couldn't comprehend how that income alone could ever get me to my goals. That's when he explained something I never forgot:

The person who begins investing early often accumulates more wealth than the person who begins later, even if the latter earns a higher income. Time, in this case, not my salary, was the biggest asset I possessed.

I intentionally placed the concept of compounding interest at the beginning of this book because it is one of the clearest explanations of how wealth is truly built.

It is not built by spending money to appear rich.

It is not built overnight.

It is not built by relying on luck.

It is built through consistency over time. Which is the fuel that powers compounding interest.

Compound interest is interest that is added to the initial principal of a deposit, investment or loan, thereby increasing the balance and in turn, increasing the amount of interest earned in the next period. In other words, it is what happens when your money makes money and then that money also goes ahead and makes more money. Savings, Money market and dividend stocks all optimize the benefits of compounding interest.

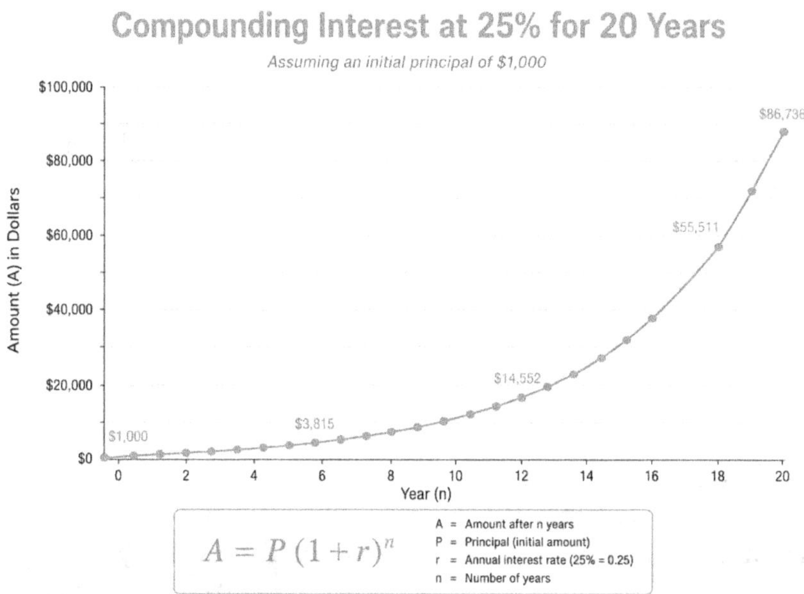

Tessy decides to invest with an initial principal of $1,000 compounding annually at a 25% rate for 20 years. Her money will grow to a total of $86,736.

The time value of money (TVM) states that money today is worth more than the same amount in the future because it can earn returns over time. Compounding is the engine that drives this. Using TVM, every year her money becomes the initial principal + returns earned on prior returns

The formula behind the chart is:

Where:

- FV = Future Value
- PV = Present Value ($1,000)
- r = annual return (25% or 0.25)

- n = number of years

Applied to Tessy's example:

After 20 years:

- $1,000 becomes about $87,000

The important note here is that the first few years will feel slow and most of her wealth creation will occur in the later years.

For example:

- Year 1 = $1,250
- Year 10 = $9,313
- Year 15 = $28,422
- Year 20 = $86,736

In year 1, she makes about $250 in interest. By year 10, her balance is now almost 10 times the initial principal. You will notice that in the last 5 years, she added almost $60,000. This is the essence of compounding. Returns are higher and increase dramatically over long periods. The curve in the chart accelerates where it starts out flat at the beginning and become steep at the end. That steepness is TVM in all its glory. This happens because returns begin to earn their own returns.

The power of compounding helps money grow faster than if only simple interest were calculated on the principal alone, and it relies heavily on time. Small, disciplined decisions made consistently over the years allow your contributions to multiply.

But compounding also relies heavily on avoiding poor decisions. As powerful as it is at growing wealth, compounding can work just as powerfully against you when you carry high interest debt.

When you have debt, the opposite happens. You are charged interest on your original balance, and then you are charged interest on the interest you haven't paid off yet.

Let's imagine Tessy holds a $1,000 balance on a credit card with a 25% APR, and she makes no payments:

Month 1: She is charged interest on the $1,000 balance. Her new balance is $1,020.83. **Month 2:** Now she isn't just charged interest on the original $1,000. She is now charged interest on $1,020.83. Her ending balance is $1,042.10. Month 3: The interest is now calculated on Month 2's ending balance. Her ending balance is $1,063.81.

In just 3 months, her debt has grown by about 6.4%. As interest is added to the balance, future interest is charged on both the original debt and the previously accrued interest. With time, this can make what was supposed to be a manageable debt increasingly difficult to repay.

One of the most valuable assets in investing is time. Consider Kiara, who decides to begins investing at the age of 25. Kiara chooses a path of early financial literacy and discipline, committing $300 monthly ($3,600 annually). Assuming a steady 10% average annual return over a 25-year horizon, her portfolio is projected to surpass $430,000 by age 50. This calculation sits on the conservative side, completely excluding any future salary increases, side business revenue, or future capacity to contribute.

Nneka, her peer, waits until age 35 to begin. She prioritizes immediate lifestyle consumption throughout her 20s, allocating her resources toward high-end rentals, luxury items, and maintaining the visual aesthetics of a "soft life." Realizing the gap at age 35, she attempts to compensate by aggressively doubling the input to $600 monthly. Despite committing significantly more capital out-of-pocket over her 15-year window, her projected portfolio at age 50 reaches only $250,000 to $300,000.

An increased monthly contribution cannot outrun a lost decade. In the mechanics of compounding, time is the ultimate leverage. Despite investing far less money, Kiara may end up with a larger portfolio at retirement because her money had an extra decade to compound.

Most people look at financial decisions and only see the money. But those dollars are just the surface layer.

At its core, every financial choice you make is an exchange of your most valuable, non-renewable resources:

- **Time & Energy:** The literal life force you expended to earn that capital, and the hours you will spend managing or worrying about it.
- **Attention:** The mental bandwidth consumed by your choices, pulling your focus toward or away from what truly matters.
- **Relationships**: How your financial habits impact your connection with partners, family, and your community.
- **Sacrifice & Future Possibilities:** What you are choosing to give up right now to unlock—or lock away—options for your future self.

Every single financial crossroad carries a dual reality: you are choosing a gain, but you are simultaneously accepting a tradeoff.

That hidden tradeoff is your true opportunity cost.

Since I majored in Economics in college, the topic of opportunity cost was not foreign to me. It was viewed more as an academic concept rather than a daily reality, but economists think of it like this:

Opportunity Cost = Value of Next Best Alternative – Value of Chosen Option

Opportunity cost is the value of what you give up in order to choose something else.

For example, purchasing a Mercedes SUV may also mean delayed investing, reduced savings, less flexibility and more financial pressure.

Staying in the wrong relationship may cost you peace, your mental health and time rebuilding yourself. Having children earlier may cost you your career growth, freedom and mobility while waiting longer to have them may cost you time and ease of fertility.

Everything has a cost, even good decisions. The reason opportunity cost matters is because our choices compound over time.

If you decide to keep $10,000 in cash for a year instead of putting it into a high-yield savings account earning 5% interest, the opportunity cost of holding cash is $500. You didn't lose cash out of your pocket, but you lost the ability to earn that $500. The opportunity cost grows because the missed interest also misses the chance to earn interest.

Year	If Invested at 5%	Opportunity Cost of Keeping Cash
1	$10,500	$500
5	$12,763	$2,763
10	$16,289	$6,289
15	$20,789	$10,789
20	$26,533	$16,533

One unnecessary expense is rarely the issue.

But years of bad debt, lifestyle inflation and inconsistencies in investing create compounded consequences.

Likewise investing wisely, building skills and choosing good relationships also compound. The basic idea is this: Your future is quietly shaped by what you repeatedly choose over what you repeatedly postpone.

2

Setting Financial Goals

"Yeah, I'm that invested, but you can't attest it
Million-dollar goals, managed to manifest it"

— BIG SEAN

The 50-30-20 Budget rule

One of the simplest budgeting frameworks I encountered was the 50-30-20 rule, popularized by Senator Elizabeth Warren and Amelia Warren Tyagi. The concept is straightforward. 50% of your income goes toward needs, the things you absolutely must pay every month: rent or mortgage, transportation and utilities like electricity, water, and gas. 30% goes toward wants, the things that improve your quality of life but are not essential to survival, dining out and shopping, entertainment, and streaming subscriptions. The remaining 20% goes toward savings, money set aside for your future and for protection against emergencies. This bucket includes retirement contributions, college savings, emergency fund deposits, and sinking funds for things like car repairs or home maintenance.

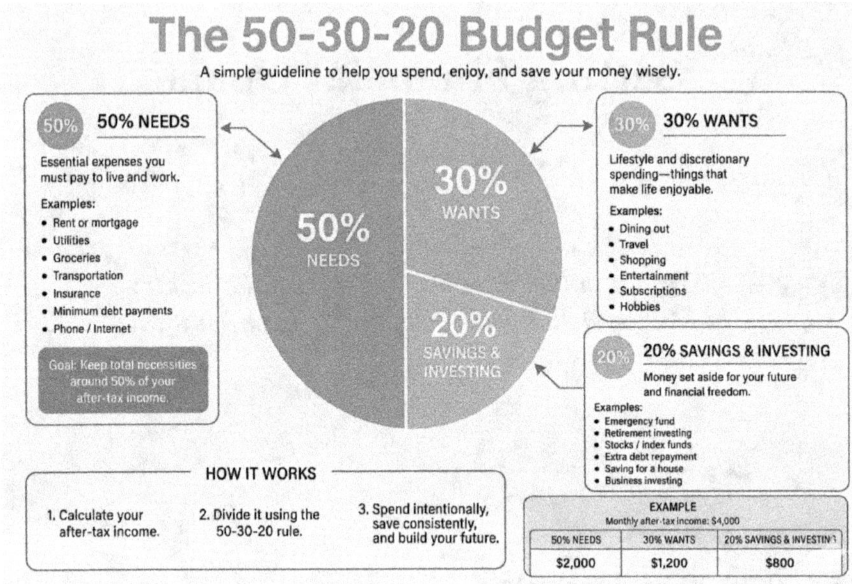

For most young people coming out of school, they may still live with their parents so some of these costs are offset by their families. For me though, starting out in New York City, every single one of these expenses fell entirely on me.

When I first came out of grad school, the average price of a one-bedroom apartment in Manhattan was about $3,500 a month. With a salary of $85,000, I was taking home about $5,500 after taxes. Once I deducted the MTA card and utilities, I would have been left with only about $500. Since I was so focused on building my savings, I quickly realized that $3,500 in rent would be too much of a burden. That analysis led me to start researching apartments outside of Manhattan, and the first place I found was a studio for about $2,500 a month.

But even with a cheaper apartment, eating out became the budget category that quietly got away from me. I always planned to grab breakfast before leaving the house but most mornings I rushed out with nothing but a banana. By 9:45 am without fail I was hungry, so I would head down to the company cafeteria for a $6 bagel. Lunch in the Manhattan area ran about $13 for a salad, and by the time I got home in the evenings I genuinely did not want to cook, so I would order from the local stores for around $20. Those daily costs added up faster than I expected. Groceries at Trader Joe's ran me about $100 a week, so just for food alone I was looking at approximately $1,200 a month, which was very different from what I had budgeted for when I first sat down with a spreadsheet.

Being in the city, transportation is easier to manage when you stick to the subway with the occasional last-minute cab or Uber thrown in. The base fare was about $2.75 per ride, a 7-day Unlimited MetroCard was $31, and a 30-day Unlimited MetroCard was $116.50. For a 25-year-old corporate worker commuting five days a week, the 30-day unlimited was almost always the most cost-effective option because you could factor in weekend outings and other impromptu trips too.

Some of my friends lived in nearby suburbs though, which meant their commute looked very different. They had to drive to the closest train station, find parking, take a commuter rail that connected them to the MTA, and then navigate the subway once they arrived in the city. That is three layers of cost before they even sat down at their desks.

Driving costs alone ran anywhere from $80 to $150 a month for gas depending on distance, plus $50 to $100 a month averaged out for car maintenance, and tolls anywhere from nothing to $200 a month depending on the route. Parking at the train station added another $40 to $120 a month for a permit, with some towns charging daily rates instead. Then came the commuter rail pass itself. In 2016, a monthly pass on the LIRR, Metro-North, or NJ Transit typically ranged from

$180 to $350 depending on how far from the city you lived. Closer suburbs like Yonkers or Jamaica ran around $180 to $220 a month, while farther spots like White Plains, Stamford, or towns out on Long Island pushed that figure to $250 and above. If the rail pass did not include subway access, which many did not, you were adding another $116.50 for a 30-day MetroCard on top of everything else. NJ Transit riders who needed the PATH train added $2.75 per ride on top of that.

When you add it all up, a suburban commuter in 2016 was easily spending several hundred dollars a month just to get to work and back, while someone living in the city paid one flat monthly transit fee and called it done.

As you start to understand how differently people spend just on transportation alone, you begin to see a bigger picture: lifestyle costs eat into salaries in ways that income figures on paper never fully capture.

Take this comparison. As a single woman with no children, your $85,000 salary may actually give you more flexibility, more savings, and more room for the things you enjoy than a married man with three children making $200,000. That might sound surprising at first, but the numbers tell the story clearly.

A married 45-year-old with three children earning $200,000 in New York City is looking at monthly expenses that can range anywhere from $10,300 on the conservative end to $22,000 or more when you factor in everything. A three-bedroom apartment or mortgage runs $4,000 to $7,500 a month. Utilities and internet add $300 to $600. Groceries for a family of five sit at $1,200 to $2,000. Dining out and family outings add $400 to $1,000. Transportation with a car and transit runs $500 to $1,200. Health insurance and medical costs come in at $800 to $1,500. And then there is childcare, school fees, and activities, which alone can run $2,000 to $5,000 or more every single month. Add life insurance, home insurance, family clothing, and retirement and college savings on top of that, and $200,000 a year in New York City with three children is not wealthy. It is financially stretched middle class.

Childcare is the single biggest wildcard in that budget. It can cost as much as $2,000 to $5,000 per month, which in many other American cities would be someone's entire salary. And if private school enters the picture, add another $3,000 to $6,000 per child per month, and everything changes overnight.

The single woman at 25 has something the family of five simply does not: flexibility. She can move apartments, cut dining out, get a roommate, shift boroughs, and adjust her lifestyle relatively quickly when she needs to. The family has far fewer levers to pull without making major life changes. Income does not scale lifestyle in a straight line. The $200,000 household does not feel two and a half times richer than the $85,000 household because costs scale with family size in ways that income alone cannot outdo.

You'll see in the family's scenario, that the 50-30-20 budgeting rule fails. Why? Because "Needs" routinely exceed 80% of Take-Home Pay. In a standard budget, childcare is sometimes tossed into the "Wants" category if it's optional, but for a working family, it is an absolute need. If housing ($4,000) and baseline childcare ($2,000) alone take up $6,000, this family has already blown past their entire 50% "Needs" allocation ($5,750) and they haven't bought a single grocery, paid a utility bill, or covered health insurance yet.

To make the numbers work, the 30% "Wants" section has to be aggressively reduced. Instead of spending $3,450 on lifestyle and fun, the family is likely spending closer to 5% or 10% on dining out and outings just to cover the deficit in the "Needs" column.

At age 45 with three kids, saving for retirement and college isn't a future luxury; it's a time-sensitive emergency. Yet, hitting the $2,300 monthly savings target (20%) is nearly impossible if expenses creep toward the mid-to-higher end of your estimates.

Since the standard rule does not apply, intentional financial planning for this scenario requires flipping the framework into a flexed budget which involves paying yourself first and securing the 20%. At 45, instead of saving what is left over, the savings goal is pulled out directly via automated 401k contributions and 529 plans before the paycheck hits the bank. This forces the family to live on the remaining 80%. Also, accepting that fixed "Needs" will consume roughly 75% to 80% of net income in NYC. The remaining 5% goes toward ruthless, hyper-intentional spending on "Wants" that keep the family sane—like a specific weekly pizza night or a shared family activity—while cutting out all mid-tier convenience spending. The $2,000 to $5,000 childcare bill has a structural expiration date. Once children enter public school, that cash flow unlocks. In an adapted budget, 100% of that reclaimed childcare money must be immediately redirected into asset protection and retirement urgency to make up for lost time, rather than allowing it to expand the lifestyle.

The point here is that a 25-year-old single earner can use 50-30-20 as a loose guide because their life has elasticity. However, for the 45-year-old family of five in NYC, the rule cannot be followed traditionally; instead of trying to force rigid, balanced percentages onto an expensive reality, the strategy must pivot entirely: survival and success mean fiercely managing heavy fixed costs while building an unshakeable wall around your savings rate.

The wealth-building paths are different too. At 25, the focus is compounding and career growth. At 45, with three children in New York City, the focus has shifted entirely to asset protection, education funding, and retirement urgency. Both are valid stages. But understanding which stage you are in and what it actually costs to live your life is what separates intentional financial planning from simply hoping the numbers work out at the end of the month.

The Influencer Path Top of Form

At my last role I worked with a 25-year-old intern who, alongside her position as a Marketing Strategist, was quietly building an influencer presence on the side. She would speak frequently about how much people underestimated what it took to become a successful creator, not just the effort but the real financial cost of getting there. So, let's look honestly at what happens to our 25-year-old's budget if she decides to add an influencer side hustle on top of her corporate job.

It can definitely shift the picture, but it is not automatically a financial upgrade. An influencer side hustle almost always starts as low or inconsistent income with significant upfront effort, especially in a city like New York where the competition is as intense as anywhere in the world.

Her take-home pay stays at around $5,000 a month from her base salary. On the income side, influencer earnings in the early months, typically the first six months, realistically run anywhere from nothing to about $200 a month. Between six and eighteen months, if growth is solid, that can rise to somewhere between $200 and $2,000 a month. Only the top ten to twenty percent of creators ever reach consistent earnings of $2,000 to $10,000 or more per month, and that is the honest reality most people do not talk about when they are selling the influencer dream online.

What people consistently underestimate is the cost side. Building a content presence in New York City is not free. Equipment like cameras, lighting, and phone upgrades runs $50 to $200 a month when amortized. Editing software and tools add $20 to $100. Clothing, aesthetics, and props can easily cost $100 to $500 a month. Experiences, the restaurants, travel, and events that create the content, add $200 to $800. Optional marketing and ads bring in another $0 to $300. All in, the influencer path adds roughly $200 to $1,500 in new monthly costs before a single dollar of income arrives. In New York City, content lifestyle spending can quietly explode before you even notice it happening.

In the early stage, which is the most realistic scenario for most people starting out, extra income runs $0 to $300 while extra costs run $300 to $800. She is actually losing money every month. As a growing creator thing start to balance out, with extra income of $500 to $2,000 against extra costs of $400 to $1,200, leaving a net gain somewhere between nothing and $800, meaningful but not yet life-changing. Only at the successful influencer stage, where income runs $3,000 to $8,000 or more and costs settle at $800 to $2,000, does the net gain become genuinely significant at $2,000 to $6,000 or more a month.

Emergency Fund

Living in New York City, I cannot count the number of random unexpected costs I ran into that I never would have anticipated before moving there. Broker fees were one of them. In New York, unlike most other cities in the country, it is common for renters to pay a broker fee just to secure an apartment, sometimes as much as one month's rent or more, even when you did not personally hire the broker. It is one of those costs nobody warns you about until you are already sitting across from a landlord with a pen in your hand.

Another expensive surprise I experienced personally was having to leave an apartment and break my lease early. The situation was not planned, and it was not optional, and what I discovered was that breaking a lease in New York City is not just an inconvenience. It is a multi-thousand-dollar financial shock that can arrive all at once.

To understand what that looks like in real numbers, imagine you are renting at $2,500 a month with five months still remaining on your lease. The lease break penalty alone typically runs one to two months' rent, so right away you are looking at $2,500 to $5,000. On top of that, many landlords will hold you responsible for rent until they find a replacement tenant, which in New York can take one to three months, adding another $2,500 to $7,500. You may lose part or all of your security deposit, which adds $1,000 to $2,500. Moving costs for movers, transport, and boxes run $300 to $1,500. And then your new apartment requires its own first month and deposit upfront, another $5,000 to $7,500 before you have even unpacked a single box.

At the low end that is around $5,000. At the high end it is $15,000 or more. And none of it arrives with much warning.

This is not the kind of situation that happens because someone was careless. Breaking a lease early is usually triggered by something real: a job loss, a relocation, an unsafe living situation, a relationship ending, or a financial crisis that forces the decision. You do not always have the luxury of time to save gradually when those things happen. That is precisely what an emergency fund is for.

Without one, the options are painful. Most people reach for credit cards and take on high interest debt. Others take out personal loans, borrow from family, or drain their retirement savings. Every one of those options creates longer-term financial damage that outlasts the original emergency by months or even years.

Even with an emergency fund in place there are ways to reduce the hit. Finding a replacement tenant yourself is the single biggest cost saver. Negotiating with your landlord early, timing your move as close to the end of the lease as possible, and keeping thorough documentation all help because New York City does have tenant protections worth knowing about.

For a 25-year-old taking home around $5,000 a month in New York City, the realistic emergency fund target sits between $10,000 and $20,000, because breaking a lease alone could wipe out two to four months of income in one go. More broadly, the two most common emergencies this demographic faces are job loss and medical costs. Three months of unemployment in New York, covering rent and basic living costs, runs $10,000 to $18,000. Medical costs, even with insurance, when you factor in deductibles, out-of-network care, and mental health expenses, typically hit somewhere between $1,000 and $6,000.

What makes this stage of life particularly vulnerable is that the safety net is thin. There are fewer savings built up, less access to credit at good rates, and life itself is more volatile: career changes, moving cities, relationship shifts. Emergencies at 25 are both more frequent and harder to absorb than they will be a decade later.

The minimum emergency fund for this profile in New York City is $8,000 to $10,000. A safer target is $12,000 to $20,000, which represents roughly three to six months of essential expenses.

And if your fixed costs are higher than average, which in New York City they very often are, the 50-30-20 rule may need to flex to reflect your reality. A 60-20-20 or even a 70-10-20 split might be what your situation actually calls for. The numbers are a guide, not a cage. What matters most is that you spend with purpose, save consistently, and never let lifestyle wants quietly swallow the goals you are working toward.

Your Personal Finance Dashboard

Most of my later career years were spent in Financial Planning & Analysis (FP&A) roles, where I learned that numbers alone rarely tell a story. A large part of these roles involved transforming financial data into clear, actionable insights for non-financial stakeholders. Using business intelligence tools, I built dashboards that tracked the organization's most important Key Performance Indicators or KPIs and regularly presented them to leadership teams. In many ways, the job was as much about communication and storytelling as it was about finance—helping people understand what the numbers meant and how they could use them to make better decisions.

Over time, I realized that the same principles companies use to manage their finances can be applied to our personal lives.

Every successful organization tracks a handful of key metrics to measure its financial health. Why should your personal finances be any different?

A woman doesn't need expensive software or a finance degree to create her own personal finance dashboard. A simple spreadsheet, budgeting app, or even a notebook can serve the same purpose. The key is identifying the personal financial KPIs that matter most to her goals.

These might include monthly income, savings rate, emergency fund balance, investment contributions, net worth, debt balance, housing costs as a percentage of income and progress toward specific financial goals.

Just as a CEO reviews a company's dashboard to understand its financial position, your personal finances deserve the same treatment. You should regularly review your own. When you track your financial health

Total Wealth & Cash Flow Dashboard

MONTHLY INCOME	MONTHLY EXPENSES	NET WORTH	DEBTS
$8,500.00	**$6,100.00**	**$185,000.00**	**$55,000.00**
Net Take-Home	Fixed & Variable Costs	Total Assets - Liabilities	Total Outstanding Balances

Net Worth Progression (12 Months)

Investment Portfolio

401(k) / Roth IRA	$120,000 (65%)
Brokerage Account	$45,000 (24%)
Real Estate Equity	$20,000 (11%)

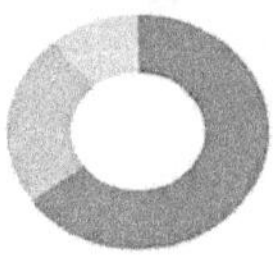

Investment Strategy Tip:
Automate your contributions and maintain a balanced portfolio

Liabilities & Reserves

Student Loans	$35,000
Car Loan	$15,000
Credit Cards	$5,000
Emergency Fund (Liquid Cash)	**$25,000** 4.1 Mo. Runway

Debt Paydown Strategy:
Prioritize high-interest loans for faster progress

3

Assets that make you rich while you sleep

"I coulda bought a place in Dumbo before it was Dumbo for like 2 million, that same building today is worth 25 million"

— JAY Z

For years I worked and searched for finance and accounting roles, negotiated salaries and built my independence but as a young, bright-eyed female in a city that I didn't grow up in, I was frequently asked, "Why are you doing all this on your own?", "Don't you have parents to help you?", "Aren't you better off in your own country where you would be supported?" The truth is I needed to know that I could do it. As the firstborn daughter, I often found myself thinking about worst-case scenarios: What if something happened? What if my parents were no longer around to support my siblings and me? Who would I have to rely on then?

That mindset pushed me toward independence. Part of it may have been a desire for control, but it was also shaped by my experiences in relationships, where I never wanted to feel dependent on someone else or have their financial support used against me. I wanted the confidence that came from knowing that I could stand on my own two feet, make my own decisions and build a life that wasn't contingent on anyone's approval or resources.

For me, independence was never about rejecting support. It was about proving to myself that I could survive, adapt and thrive on my own if I ever had to.

Eventually, I realized that true independence isn't just about earning income. It's about building assets that continue to work for you long after you've logged off, gone to sleep, or taken a break. Wealth isn't created solely by working harder; it's created by owning things that generate value even when you're not actively involved.

The biggest financial breakthrough of my life did not come from a promotion, a salary negotiation, or even an investment.

It came from understanding the difference between earning money and owning assets.

For most of our lives, we are taught to focus on income, study hard, build a career, increase our earnings, and find better opportunities. None of this advice is wrong.

In fact, income is often the foundation upon which financial security is built.

The problem is that income alone has limitations.

No matter how talented, ambitious, or hardworking someone is, there are still only twenty-four hours in a day. Income earned through work remains connected to time, energy, and presence. A promotion may increase your earnings. A new job may improve your circumstances. Additional qualifications may open new doors. Yet the underlying arrangement remains largely the same: you are exchanging a portion of your life for a paycheck.

There is a ceiling to that model.

Assets operate differently.

An asset is something that continues creating value after the initial effort, capital, or resources have been invested. Unlike employment income, an asset does not require your constant participation to produce results. It can continue generating returns while you are sleeping, spending time with family, traveling, caring for loved ones, pursuing other opportunities, or simply taking a break.

That distinction may sound subtle, but it changes the way you think about money entirely.

Security comes from income.

Independence comes from ownership.

The women who build lasting wealth were not necessarily the highest earners. Many earned good incomes, but what truly separated them was how they spent the money once it arrived. Rather than allowing every increase in income to flow directly into lifestyle upgrades, they gradually converted earned income into productive assets.

They bought investments and acquired ownership stakes.

They built systems that could continue creating value long after the original work had been completed.

The goal is not to stop working but to ensure that your money learns how to work alongside you.

Rental Income

When people hear "rental income", they often assume it's something reserved for the already wealthy. For many young professionals, it can actually be one of the first assets that generates income while they sleep.

Take Adanna, a 27-year-old corporate lawyer working in New York City. She earns a good salary, saves consistently, and instead of upgrading her lifestyle every time she gets a raise or bonus and directs a portion of her income toward purchasing a rental property. She buys a small duplex for $350,000, puts down 20%, and finances the rest. To offset the mortgage payment, property taxes, and maintenance costs, she decides to live in one unit and rent out the other.

Over time, that one decision sets off a quiet chain of events that builds her wealth on autopilot. Every month she clears a few hundred dollars in cash flow after all expenses are paid. It may not look like wealth at first, but that money shows up consistently whether she is at her desk, on a beach, or fast asleep. As rental rates rise with inflation over the years, her income from the property grows while her mortgage payment stays exactly the same. The property itself appreciates in value, so if the market pushes it to $450,000 she has gained $100,000 in net worth without doing a single thing to earn it. And every rent payment her tenant makes chips away at the mortgage balance, which means her tenant is quietly building equity on her behalf every single month.

By the time Adanna is 37, she owns a property worth more than she paid for it, collects higher rent than when she started, carries a lower mortgage balance, and generates more income than she did in year one. Down the line, she can pass that property to her children or sell it and pass down the capital instead. That is where generational wealth actually gets created. But it only works if she does not overspend the savings, maintains the property properly, and makes smart decisions along the way.

The apartment just exists and creates wealth, with no boss, no fixed hours, and no daily operations required. But low effort does not mean no responsibility, and it is worth being honest about that.

Most of the time the engine runs quietly in the background. But any seasoned investor will tell you there are inevitable moments when effort is necessary. An appliance breaks and needs an immediate fix. A tenant issue arises and drains both your time and your emotional energy. An unexpected building assessment lands on your desk, bringing high, unbudgeted costs. And underneath all of that is the ongoing baseline of paperwork: taxes, insurance, and bookkeeping that never fully goes away.

A property only stays low effort if you follow three rules without exception. The building must be well managed. The property must be meticulously maintained. And you must never over-leverage or neglect the asset. Fail on any one of those fronts and what was supposed to be a hands-off investment becomes a stressful, time-consuming second job. But manage those risks properly and the math behind property ownership becomes one of the most powerful wealth-building engines available to you.

Anatomy of a $350,000 Investment

To understand how this works in practice, let's look at the anatomy of a standard residential purchase. Imagine you find a strong investment property priced at $350,000.

Getting into the game requires real capital upfront. You are not just covering the purchase price. You need a 20% down payment of $70,000, plus closing costs of around $10,000, which brings your total upfront cash requirement to approximately $80,000.

Once you own the deed, the monthly carrying costs include your mortgage on the remaining $280,000 loan, which runs $1,700 to $2,000 a month, property taxes and insurance at $400 to $700, and a maintenance reserve set aside as a standard rule of thumb. All in, your total monthly outflow sits between $2,300 and $3,100.

On the income side, depending on the town, the property type, and its condition, a $350,000 asset will typically command monthly rent of $2,400 to $3,200.

Now here is where it gets interesting. In a conservative scenario where you collect $2,500 in rent but your monthly costs run on the higher side at $2,700, your cash flow on paper is negative by $200. To someone looking only at that number it looks like a losing investment. But that surface reading misses the real mechanics entirely. Behind the scenes a three-pronged wealth engine is running in your favor regardless of that monthly $200 gap. Your tenant's rent is paying down your mortgage balance every single month. The property is appreciating in value over time. And your equity position is growing from both sides simultaneously.

The power of leverage is what makes this so compelling. You only put in $80,000 of your own cash, yet you are capturing the growth and principal paydown on a $350,000 asset. Generating a $15,000 to $30,000 annual increase in net worth on an $80,000 cash investment is a return that very few other asset classes can come close to matching.

Real wealth in real estate isn't built by owning a single property. It is built by scaling the model over time, and once you understand how it works you can treat it as a repeatable process.

In the first three years, the focus is entirely on execution. You buy your first property, place a qualified tenant, optimize your systems, and stabilize the rental. You learn how to handle the inevitable effort spikes without panicking, and you build the confidence that comes from seeing the model actually work.

Between years three and five, inflation and market demand begin lifting the value of the property while your tenant's monthly payments steadily chip away at your loan balance. Your equity position is growing from both sides at once. At this point you either harvest that equity through a refinance or continue building your cash reserves.

Between years five and ten, the equity and cash reserves from your first property give you the capital for a down payment on a second. You purchase the next asset, apply the same management systems you have already built, and repeat the process from the beginning.

By compounding your returns and using leverage wisely, a single upfront investment of $80,000 becomes the starting point for a multi-property portfolio that can secure genuine financial independence.

Real estate is often described as one of the most powerful wealth-building tools available, and for good reason. It combines leverage, appreciation, cash flow, and equity growth in a way few assets can match.

However, one of the most common mistakes investors make is assuming that every financial goal should be solved with property.

The reality is that every asset class has strengths and limitations.

Real estate can create substantial wealth, but it also requires capital, ongoing management, and patience.

A property cannot be sold as easily as a share in a publicly traded company. Unexpected repairs can affect returns. Market conditions can influence rental demand. These limitations do not make real estate a poor investment. They simply remind us that no single asset should carry the entire responsibility for our financial future.

Stocks

For a long time, I followed the traditional rulebook: work hard, save what i can, and trade my time for a paycheck. But I eventually realized that relying solely on my own hours put a ceiling on my potential, after all, there are only so many hours in a day. That all changed when I discovered the stock market. It shifted my entire mindset from just being an employee to becoming an owner. Investing showed me that I could put my money to work in businesses that run 24/7, creating a stream of value that grows even when I'm logged off. I want to share how shifting from a mindset of consumption to one of ownership has completely transformed my view of financial freedom.

The phrase "making money while you sleep" is one of the most overused cliches in personal finance. Yet, when applied to the stock market, it becomes a literal description of how wealth accumulation works.

To truly understand this concept, you must look past the flashing tickers and complex financial jargon. At its core, buying a stock—whether it is a single share of Apple, Microsoft, or a broad index fund—means you are purchasing a fractional ownership stake in a living, breathing business. While you are sleeping, eating, or working your day job, these corporations are actively designing products, closing deals, generating profits, and expanding their global footprints.

The market does not provide a guaranteed paycheck every single night. Instead, it serves as a vehicle for continuous compounding and macroeconomic growth that functions entirely independent of your daily labor.

This distinction is important because most people approach money through the lens of effort-to-income. You work, you get paid. You stop working, income stops. The stock market breaks that direct link between time and earnings.

When you deploy capital into equities, your wealth grows through three distinct interlocking mechanisms.

The first is price appreciation. As a business becomes more efficient and successful its revenue and profits rise, and as those fundamentals improve the market assigns a higher valuation to the company, causing the share price to climb. A baseline investment of $10,000 placed into a diversified portfolio growing at the historic average of 7% annually becomes approximately $20,000 after ten years, $40,000 after twenty years, and $76,000 after thirty years. You did not have to clock in, manage employees, or manufacture a single product to achieve any of that growth. The underlying businesses did the heavy lifting while your capital quietly compounded in the background. This is where ownership separates itself from income. Income requires presence. Ownership does not.

The second mechanism is dividends. While some companies reinvest all their earnings back into growth, mature companies like Coca-Cola and Procter & Gamble regularly distribute a portion of their profits directly back to their investors. These cash payments, usually distributed quarterly, are the closest thing to true passive cash flow that the stock market offers. You receive real money simply for holding the asset.

The third mechanism is reinvestment, and this is where the real power lives. By enrolling in a Dividend Reinvestment Plan, known as a DRIP, your quarterly dividend payouts are automatically used to purchase more shares. More shares generate larger dividends, which purchase even more shares. It becomes a self-feeding loop, and over long periods of time that loop is what drives genuinely exponential growth.

To see what this looks like in practice, take Maya, who commits to saving $500 a month starting at age 25, assuming a conservative average annual return of 7%. At the 20-year mark, when she is 45, she has contributed $120,000 of her own money and her portfolio has grown to approximately $260,000. The early decades are steady but modest, her personal contributions doing most of the heavy lifting. By the 40-year mark, when she is 65, she has contributed $240,000 total and her portfolio has grown to approximately $1,200,000. She doubled her contributions but her wealth more than quadrupled. Most of Maya's lifetime growth happens in those later years, when the snowball has grown large enough that its own momentum generates far more wealth than her monthly contributions ever could.

Understanding the math of compounding is only half the battle. You must also have the psychological steadiness to withstand market volatility, and that is a very different kind of skill. Warren Buffett captured the duality of market cycles in one of his most quoted observations:

"Money is made when the market is rising; wealth is made when the market is falling."

When the market is moving upward, generating returns feels almost effortless. A rising tide lifts all boats, momentum carries the broader market higher, and investors enjoy seeing their account balances climb. But true wealth is built during the downturns. When stock prices fall, amateur investors panic and sell. Seasoned investors look at the same moment and see a sale on world-class companies at a steep discount.

In 2008, during the Global Financial Crisis, stock markets worldwide plunged, major financial institutions failed, and investors watched years of progress disappear almost overnight. And yet what was remarkable was that while stock prices were falling, the underlying reality of ownership had not changed. Businesses were still operating. Consumers still needed goods and services. Those who panicked and sold, locked in their losses permanently. Those who stayed the course and kept contributing to their portfolios were positioned to benefit fully from the recovery that followed.

That is the nature of markets: a peak, a decline, and eventually a recovery. No season lasts forever. The investors who understand that tend to be the ones still standing when everyone else has given up.

Real Estate vs Stocks: Asset Comparison

Factor	Real Estate	Stocks
Passive income	Rent	Dividends
Capital growth	Property appreciation	Share price appreciation
Effort required	Medium–High	Very Low
Liquidity	Low (months to sell)	High (seconds to sell)
Entry cost	High deposit/down payment	Can start with small amounts
Diversification	Harder	Easy through index funds
Leverage	Common via mortgages	Limited for most investors
Ongoing costs	Maintenance, taxes, insurance	Minimal for index funds
Volatility	Less visible day-to-day	Prices fluctuate daily
Scalability	Slower	Easier to scale investments

Digital Assets

Cryptocurrencies

The rise of Bitcoin introduced a fundamentally new way of thinking about wealth. Unlike a stock it does not pay dividends, and unlike a property it does not generate rent. But many investors are drawn to its potential for long-term appreciation and the fact that it operates entirely outside the traditional financial system.

For most people the most powerful way to build wealth with Bitcoin is not trading it actively or trying to time the market. It is simply owning it and letting time do the work. Rather than watching price charts and searching for the perfect moment to buy, you can automate a fixed investment amount at regular intervals, perhaps fifty dollars every payday. This approach is known as dollar-cost averaging, or DCA, and what it does is smooth out the impact of market volatility over time. Because you are buying at regular intervals regardless of the price, you naturally buy more when prices are low and less when they are high, which averages out your cost basis in a way that consistent timing rarely achieves.

After each purchase, the recommended practice is to transfer your Bitcoin to cold storage, which is an offline hardware device that keeps your digital assets completely secure from cyber threats. With your investments automated and your assets safely stored, you stop being a short-term trader reacting to every market move and become a long-term investor focused on steady, patient wealth accumulation. Your portfolio continues working in the background while you get on with the rest of your life, which is exactly the point of building assets that do not require your constant attention to function.

Digital Products

The idea behind digital products is simple and genuinely powerful: you build something once and sell it an unlimited number of times. Ebooks, online courses, Notion templates, stock photography, all of these can be listed on global marketplaces like Etsy, Gumroad, or Amazon and generate income around the clock without you being present for a single transaction. There is no inventory to manage, no shipping costs, and no physical overhead. The product exists, the marketplace handles the sale, and the money arrives while you are doing something else entirely.

Content Platforms

YouTube channels, niche blogs, and evergreen websites work on a similar principle. The upfront investment is time and effort, often significant effort, but once that content is established it generates revenue for years through a combination of advertising, affiliate commissions, and brand sponsorships. A single well-researched article or video can continue earning long after the day it was published, which is what makes content a genuine long-term asset rather than just a marketing tool.

Affiliate Marketing

Affiliate marketing is one of the most accessible entry points into passive income. The model is straightforward: you promote someone else's product and earn a percentage of every sale that comes through your link. This works across blog posts, social media content, YouTube videos, and dedicated review websites. Programs like Amazon Associates give creators access to one of the most trusted retail platforms in the world. The heavy lifting happens at the beginning, building the audience, optimizing for search, and structuring the content, but once that foundation is in place the sales happen on their own.

Software and Apps

Building software represents the highest tier of digital leverage. A mobile app, a SaaS platform, or a specialized automation tool can be distributed globally through the Apple App Store or Google Play Store and scaled to thousands of users at virtually no additional cost per user. Monetization usually takes the form of monthly subscriptions or one-time purchases. The initial build requires serious investment of time, skill, and capital, but once the product is deployed the economics shift dramatically. It is worth being honest that software is rarely fully passive since ongoing maintenance, security updates, and compatibility work are always required, but the scalability it offers is unlike almost anything else in the digital economy.

The holy grail of modern entrepreneurship lies in assets you build once but sell infinitely. Think of digital products like ebooks, online courses, Notion templates or stock photography. When listed on global marketplaces like Etsy, Gumroad, or Amazon, these assets unlock a level of financial freedom that traditional businesses simply cannot match.

Why do they work so well? Because they completely eliminate physical constraints. There is no inventory to manage, no shipping feees and no overhead. You gain infinite scalability, allowing you to sell to thousands of customers simultaneously while automated systems process transactions 24/7.

Businesses that Scale

Rebecca wakes up at 2:00 AM to a notification on her phone. It's a receipt for a transaction. While she was deep in REM sleep, someone halfway across the world bought her product. She didn't have to pick up the phone, she didn't have to pack a box, and she didn't have to trade a single minute of her life to make that dollar.

Now, contrast that with being at a traditional 9-5. If she doesn't show up at the office tomorrow, her income drops to zero. She becomes a financial hostage to her own hours. The difference between these two worlds isn't how hard she works; it's a single structural concept called *scalability*. If your income has a ceiling tied to your physical time, you aren't building wealth, you are just renting out your life.

Scalability is defined by a simple economic reality: the ability to increase revenue exponentially while increasing operational costs only linearly. A truly scalable enterprise exhibits at least one of four fundamental pillars: low marginal costs (where duplicating the product costs next to nothing), robust automation (where software replaces human labor), repeatable sales frameworks (such as subscription models), and operational leverage (utilizing technology, human capital, or financial assets to multiply output).

Enterprises like Salesforce and Shopify represent the highest tier of scalability. The engineering team builds the core codebase once, and the organization can subsequently sell it to millions of users. Because the marginal cost to serve user number 1,000 versus user number 1 is nearly zero, the profit margins expand dramatically over time. Utilizing automated monthly billing and cloud infrastructure, the product operates and monetizes continuously without manual intervention.

Physical product businesses scale by decoupling the founder from logistics. By leveraging platforms like Shopify paired with outsourced fulfillment ecosystems like Amazon FBA, order processing, warehousing, and logistics are entirely automated. Because the business owner is removed from the assembly line, the storefront operates globally, processing transactions across every time zone simultaneously.

Content assets, including product review portals, comparison engines, and highly specialized niche blogs, scale via automated media. Once digital content achieves stable search engine rankings or organic traffic pipelines, the conversion path—moving a visitor from traffic to clicks to passive commissions—is fully mechanized.

Traditional brick-and-mortar operations, such as Burger King's or LifeTime Fitness, scale through rigid, documented playbooks. By converting operations into repeatable systems, the day-to-day management is handed over to staff and managers, allowing the founder to step back entirely and collect location profits or recurring franchise fees.

The Strategic Blueprint for Wealth

For professionals navigating the early stages of their career, the most reliable path to financial independence is not to abandon stability for reckless entrepreneurship. Instead, the optimal blueprint requires a three-way approach: maintain a stable primary income stream to cover foundational expenses, consistently allocate capital to broad-market equities to build passive long-term wealth, and direct residual creative energy toward building a single, scalable asset on the side. This strategy provides a crucial safety net while preserving exponential financial upside.

4

The wealthy teach this to their kids early

"Floss a little; invest up in a mutual fund"

— **BUSTA RHYMES**

The Rothschild family is one of the most studied examples of multigenerational wealth in history. What began in the late 18th century as a modest money-lending operation in Frankfurt, Germany grew under Mayer Amschel Rothschild into a banking empire that stretched across five of Europe's most powerful financial cities: London, Paris, Frankfurt, Vienna, and Naples, each branch run by one of his five sons. At the height of their influence in the 19th century, the Rothschilds were widely considered the wealthiest family in the world, and their methods were as deliberate as their ambition.

What set them apart was not simply the money they accumulated but the systems they built to protect and grow it across generations. They were known for their strict commitment to privacy, keeping their financial activities closely guarded so that neither rivals nor partners could fully grasp the scale of their wealth or the details of their strategies. They kept marriages largely within trusted circles for generations, which helped consolidate rather than dilute family capital. They communicated through private networks at a time when information itself was a form of currency. And they built one of the most extensive advisor networks of their era, surrounding themselves with lawyers, diplomats, and financial minds who helped them navigate governments, wars, and market collapses that destroyed lesser fortunes entirely.

In an era before modern financial regulation and instant communication, that discretion was not just a preference. It was a competitive advantage that compounded over time the same way money does.

Affluent families tend to prioritize teaching their heirs about managing wealth, developing business insight, and maintaining discretion from an early age. By embedding these values before the next generation is old enough to make expensive mistakes, they increase the likelihood that the family's assets will be protected rather than squandered. Descendants of John D. Rockefeller were taught structured philanthropy, financial discipline, and the stewardship of wealth as core family values. Several of the world's most enduring wealthy families maintain dedicated family offices whose entire purpose is internal financial education, providing mentorship, hands-on business involvement, and structured exposure to investment decision-making long before the next generation inherits anything.

Learn to Preserve Money, Not Just Spend It

The first and perhaps most fundamental lesson wealthy families pass down is this: money is not for spending. It is for stewarding.

From a young age, children in these households are introduced to concepts that most people do not encounter until adulthood, if ever. Budgeting, the difference between assets and liabilities, compound interest, diversification, and the mathematics of long-term growth are not abstract school subjects. They are dinner table conversations. Many families go further by giving children small stakes in family businesses or investment portfolios to manage under supervision, because there is no classroom that teaches accountability the way real consequences do.

Rather than receiving unrestricted spending money, heirs in wealthy families typically receive allowances tied directly to responsibilities or achievements. This teaches something that cannot be learned from a textbook: that wealth is connected to effort and stewardship, not to luck or entitlement. Children are made aware early that reckless spending does not just affect them personally. It affects the family's reputation, its relationships, and its ability to operate across generations.

Invest early

Wealthy families introduce their children to investing long before most people ever open a brokerage account. Property ownership is often one of the first lessons. Young heirs are shown how rental homes and commercial real estate generate income and appreciate over time, and more importantly they are shown how holding an asset for decades consistently outperforms the temptation to flip it quickly. They learn the tax implications of property ownership, how deductions work, how trusts and LLCs can legally shield assets, and how family partnerships can be structured to optimize returns across generations. Real estate also teaches diversification in a way that feels tangible, because it is an asset class that behaves differently from stocks and bonds and reduces the risk of having everything tied to one type of market.

Beyond real estate, many wealthy families teach children about alternative assets: art, antiques, rare watches, and collectibles that appreciate quietly over decades. The lesson here is that not all value is obvious. A painting that seems like an extravagant purchase today may be worth multiples of its original price a generation from now. Grandpa Mark showing his grandson a canvas he bought forty years ago that has since multiplied in value is not just a story about money. It is a masterclass in patience and in the kind of long-term thinking that does not come naturally to most people but can be taught early.

Heirs learn to study rarity and authenticity, to understand how a watchmaker's reputation, a limited edition, or historical context drives value in ways that earnings reports never capture. They learn that unlike stocks these assets rarely pay dividends, but that their value grows steadily for those willing to hold them. Families use alternative assets to reinforce one of the most important financial habits there is: the discipline to hold, wait for the right moment, and resist the impulse to sell too soon.

Your network is tied to your net worth.

Established wealthy families rarely purchase through public markets. They access off-market real estate, private business stakes, and estate assets through relationships that have been built and maintained over years, sometimes decades. In those situations, having the right connection is often more valuable than having the capital, because the opportunity never becomes public in the first place.

Children in these environments learn this not through lectures but through proximity. They grow up overhearing conversations between adults who run companies, make investments, and hold real influence. They attend events. They watch how introductions are made and how alliances are maintained. They absorb the difference between making friends and building alliances long before they could articulate what that difference means.

One of the earliest lessons is the power of a warm introduction. Being introduced to someone by a mutual contact carries a weight that a cold outreach never can, because you inherit a portion of the trust that already exists between the introducer and the person being introduced. Wealthy families emphasize this because they understand that connections are not equal. It is not just who you know. It is the pathway through which you reach them.

Reputation is another lesson that gets taught early, and it maps directly onto the compounding principle from Chapter 1. Just as money grows on itself over time, so does trust. If you are known as reliable, generous with introductions, and genuinely useful to the people around you, your name gets passed along in rooms you have never entered. Wealthy families protect reputation with the same seriousness they protect capital, because the two are directly linked.

The deeper lesson is that strong networks are not built on charm or likability alone. They are built on mutual value. The adults that children observe are sharing opportunities, making introductions, solving problems for one another. That teaches reciprocity, the understanding that a relationship is an exchange rather than a one-way benefit, and that the most valuable thing you can bring to any network is genuine usefulness.

What all of this creates is access: access to information that never becomes public, to opportunities that are offered to trusted people before they are ever advertised, and to a faster form of trust that would otherwise take years to build independently. This is why two people with identical qualifications and identical skills can end up with profoundly different outcomes. One of them had a network. The other had a resume.

Ownership

Most people are taught to trade time for money. Get a job, earn a salary, repeat. Ownership flips that entirely. If you own part of a business, your income comes from profits rather than hours worked. Owning shares of Apple means you benefit from that company's growth and earnings without ever setting foot in one of their offices. That is a fundamentally different relationship with money than most people are ever taught to have.

The concepts that come with ownership, equity which is your slice of a business, dividends which are profits paid directly to owners, and capital gains which are increases in the value of what you own, are not complicated ideas. They are just ideas that most people are never introduced to early enough for them to matter.

Ownership also means building assets that generate income while you are not actively working. Real estate that produces rent, stocks that grow and pay dividends, businesses that operate without your daily involvement. This is what people mean when they talk about passive income, not doing anything and getting rich, but setting up systems that continue producing value long after the initial work is done. Over time those returns compound, which is why starting early is so much more powerful than starting with more money later.

Beyond the financial dimension, ownership is about control. If you own part of something you may have a say in how it is run. Wealthy families teach children to ask three questions about every situation they encounter: who owns this, who makes the decisions, and how do I get a seat at the table. Even partial ownership can translate into real influence, particularly in private businesses where decisions are made by people not committees.

The mindset shift that ownership creates goes deeper than the financial mechanics. Owners think differently about money. Instead of spending income on consumption, they redirect a portion of it consistently into acquiring more assets. Not because they do not enjoy spending, but because growing the base of what they own comes first. Buy things that can pay you back or appreciate, not just things that depreciate the moment you walk out of the store.

Ownership also introduces leverage, the concept of using other people's money, time, or skills to grow what you own. Borrowing to buy property, hiring people to scale a business, partnering to expand faster. Used wisely, leverage accelerates growth in ways that would be impossible through personal effort alone. Used carelessly, it magnifies losses just as dramatically, which is a part of the conversation that a lot of wealth advice leaves out entirely.

And underneath all of it is the lesson that ownership rewards patience in a way that a salary never can. A salary stops the moment you stop working. An asset can grow for decades after the decision to acquire it was made. That is why wealthy families teach their children to hold rather than sell, to think in decades rather than quarters, and to treat their assets with the same long-term seriousness they bring to everything else that matters.

Comfortability with risk and failure

Comfort with risk and failure is not about being reckless. It is about having a calibrated relationship with uncertainty, and in many wealthy households, children absorb this naturally because they grow up watching adults treat risk as something to be managed and understood rather than avoided at all costs.

The first shift is in how failure is framed. Instead of "you failed so you are not good enough," the question becomes "what did this teach you?" That reframe is not just motivational language. It has real consequences for behavior. People who treat outcomes as feedback make better long-term decisions than people who avoid action entirely just to protect their sense of self. When failure is normalized, you try more things, you recover faster, and you stop overreacting to setbacks. The result is not fewer failures. It is more attempts, and more attempts statistically produces more success.

The second shift is in how risk itself is evaluated. Rather than experiencing risk as one large frightening leap, wealthy families teach children to break it down into manageable questions. What is the downside? Can we absorb it? What is the upside? How do we reduce our exposure? That is essentially thinking in terms of expected value, weighing potential gains against potential losses rather than defaulting to safety out of fear. And the key insight within that framework is that not all risks are equal. Some risks are asymmetric, meaning the downside is small and contained while the upside is significant. Those are worth taking. Others carry a large downside and a limited upside. Those are worth avoiding. Learning to tell the difference is one of the most valuable financial skills there is.

There is also a behavioral element that rarely gets discussed honestly. When you grow up in an environment where a single mistake will not ruin you financially or socially, you are simply more willing to experiment. You attempt entrepreneurship earlier. You negotiate more confidently. You ask for more without the paralysis of "what if it goes wrong?" That is not just confidence. It is context. Remove the fear of catastrophic downside and behavior changes dramatically.

Children who are exposed early to businesses, investments, and real financial decisions develop an intuition for uncertainty that cannot be taught in a classroom. Risk stops being abstract and becomes something they know how to read and navigate. They develop not just risk tolerance but risk judgment, the ability to know when to push, when to walk away, and when to double down.

The identity piece matters too. If your sense of self is tied to never failing, you will avoid every situation where failure is possible. But if your identity is built around being someone who figures things out, failure becomes survivable and even useful. Wealthier environments tend to reinforce the second identity because status in those circles is not destroyed by a single bad move and bouncing back is simply expected.

It is worth being honest about where this mindset goes wrong though. Without proper grounding, it can lead to underestimating real risk because past consequences have always been cushioned, to confusing luck with skill, or to taking outsized bets without truly understanding the downside. The healthy version of this is not blind confidence. It is informed risk-taking with a clear-eyed awareness of what losing actually looks like.

How Systems work

When wealthy families talk about teaching children how systems work, they do not mean memorizing theory. They mean developing an understanding of the invisible machinery behind how money, power, and decisions actually move. It is the difference between seeing the surface of something, a job, a company, a government, and understanding the underlying incentives, rules, and leverage points that determine who wins and who does not.

Most people interact with systems as users. You apply for a job, pay your taxes, buy products, and accept the terms presented to you. Systems thinking asks a different set of questions entirely. Who designed this? What incentives are built into it? Where are the bottlenecks, and where are the advantages? Applied to something as ordinary as a job search, that shift changes everything. Instead of simply sending applications, you start asking how salaries are decided, who has the discretion to negotiate, and what signals the decision-makers respond to beyond a resume. That one reframe changes what you do and how you position yourself.

Incentives are at the center of this education. The core lesson is that people do not primarily respond to rules or intentions. They respond to incentives. Employees optimize for promotions and bonuses. Companies optimize for profit and growth metrics. Politicians optimize for re-election. Once you understand what a person or institution is optimizing for, you can often predict their behavior far more accurately than if you take their stated intentions at face value. Wealthy families expose children to these conversations explicitly, so they develop the habit of asking not just what someone says but what they are incentivized to do.

There is also a gap between the official rules and how decisions are actually made. Hiring is a clean example. Officially, the process is merit-based: qualifications, fair evaluation, best candidate wins. In reality, referrals carry enormous weight, timing matters, internal politics shape decisions, and perceived cultural fit often outweighs credentials. Neither version is dishonest, but one is incomplete. Children who grow up around decision-makers learn both layers early, which is a significant navigational advantage for the rest of their lives.

Every system also has gatekeepers, people who control access, often informally and without a title that signals it. The useful question is not "what do I need to succeed here?" It is "who actually decides, what do they care about, and how do I get in front of them?" That is a structural question rather than a social one, and it tends to produce much more useful answers.

Systems also reinforce themselves through feedback loops. A positive loop looks like this: money generates investment, investment generates returns, returns generate more investment. A negative loop looks like this: debt generates interest, interest grows the balance, a larger balance generates more interest. Recognizing which loop you are in, or which loop a decision will put you in, is one of the most practically useful things systems thinking teaches.

Real life is not one system but many overlapping ones: financial, legal, educational, social. Wealthy families tend to have exposure across several of them simultaneously, which means their children grow up seeing how these systems interact. Legal structure affects tax outcomes. Social connections shape business opportunities. Educational credentials affect network access. Seeing those connections is an advantage that is very difficult to manufacture later in life if it was not built early.

The practical application of all of this is straightforward even if the habit takes time to build. When something affects you, ask how the system behind it works. Look for the incentives rather than the stated rules. Identify who benefits and how. Over time those questions reveal patterns, and once you can see the patterns, systems that once felt opaque start to feel navigable.

5

Habits that build wealth quietly

"...Put some respect on my check/Or pay me in equity
Watch me reverse out of debt"

-- **BEYONCE**

Not every wealth-building habit is dramatic. Some of the most financially successful people are not constantly announcing new deals, posting luxury purchases, or trying to appear wealthy. For a long time, I thought building wealth required a master plan, an elite finance degree, or a lifestyle that never turned off. I assumed that "making it" meant being the busiest person in every room, constantly tethered to a laptop or a ringing phone.

Then, I met Magda.

We ended up sharing a small wooden table at a cramped local coffee shop on a random Tuesday afternoon. She was 55, wearing a faded polo shirt and a pair of beat-up sneakers, comfortably sipping a black coffee. She didn't look like a tycoon. She had no jewelry on; no Hermes bag and her hair was tied back in a messy bun. But as we got to talking, I learned she owned multiple successful businesses in the NYC area and had a net worth most people only dream of.

Yet, as the clock ticked closer to 3:00 PM, she wasn't checking stock tickers or rushing off to a board meeting. She was casually checking her watch because it was almost time to go pick up her granddaughter from elementary school.

"The businesses run smoothly because I built them to operate without me," she told me, completely unbothered by the mid-day rush. "My time belongs to me now. That's the only reason I built any of it."

That was my "aha" moment. True wealth wasn't about looking rich, and it certainly wasn't about working yourself into the ground forever. True wealth was Magda having the absolute freedom to spend her Tuesday afternoon exactly how she wanted.

When I asked her how she got there, she didn't give me a complex breakdown of market logistics. Instead, her advice mapped back to a few deceptively simple, quiet habits that anyone can start practicing today.

1. Listen and Learn From People Who Have Gone Ahead of You

One of the most underrated wealth habits is learning from people who have already seen the future before you do. This could be through mentors, books, podcasts, or financial advisors, but sometimes the most powerful version of this habit is simply observing the people around you who have spent years mastering an industry, making mistakes, and quietly identifying opportunities that nobody else noticed.

I saw this firsthand through a friend's father, a man who built a successful commercial real estate empire without ever wearing a flashy suit or making a scene.

Growing up, I watched him navigate the market with a calm precision that stood in stark contrast to the loud, frantic "hustle culture" we see online today. He didn't check tickers every five minutes, and he certainly wasn't chasing the latest trendy asset. Instead, he spent his time doing something much quieter: he watched, he listened, and he waited for the right data to line up.

One afternoon, over a casual conversation at his kitchen table, he shared a piece of wisdom that completely rewrote how I view money. He told me about a massive financial misstep he made in his late twenties, a deal he rushed into purely out of FOMO, fear of missing out. It cost him dearly, but it taught him a lesson that no textbook could replicate: the market always rewards patience and penalizes impatience. He didn't let the mistake break him. Instead, he studied the industry. He learned how contracts worked. He built relationships. He networked intentionally. And over time he quietly developed a strong list of contacts and potential clients that became the foundation of everything that came after.

He used that exact scar tissue to identify the massive undervalued opportunities that defined his career a decade later.

True financial literacy isn't about being the loudest person in the room or pretending to have all the answers. It's about having the humility to treat the world as your classroom. The most valuable wealth-building insights are rarely broadcast in a 60-second video clip. They are earned through years of discipline, trial, and error, and they are right there for the taking if you are quiet enough to notice.

Sometimes your current job is not your final destination. It may simply be training ground for your future business, investments, or ownership opportunities. Pay attention to what your industry is teaching you. Learn how money moves. Learn who the key players are. Learn where future opportunities may emerge. And most importantly, learn from people whose lives offer lessons you may need later.

Wealth often comes to people who are paying attention long before opportunity arrives.

2. Pay Yourself First

Before paying bills, before shopping, before lifestyle upgrades, pay yourself first.

This means automatically setting aside money for savings, investments, retirement accounts, or business growth before spending on anything else. Most people do it the other way around. They spend first and save whatever happens to be left, which for most people is nothing.

Wealth builders save first and adjust their lifestyle around what remains. A lot of people tell themselves they will start saving once they earn more. But for most people higher income simply creates higher spending, and the gap between what comes in and what gets saved stays exactly the same regardless of the number on the paycheck.

Imagine Tania who earns $5,000 a month. She tells herself she'll save whatever is left at the end of the month. But by week three, the money is gone. She has spent $1,200 on new clothes, $800 eating out, $500 on beauty treatments, and $400 on random online shopping, not to mention the smaller impulse buys she can barely even remember making. By the time the next payday arrives there is absolutely nothing left to show for a full month of work.

Now compare that to Eileen who has mastered paying herself first. The exact day her salary hits her account, automatic transfers route her money into dedicated buckets before she has a chance to touch it. One thousand dollars straight into investments. Five hundred into long-term savings. Five hundred into an emergency fund. Only after her financial future is secured does she touch a single dollar for lifestyle expenses. That simple flip forces her to live intentionally on what remains rather than treating her own financial freedom as an afterthought.

If you are working to recover from impulsive spending habits, automation is your best boundary. Set up automatic transfers to trigger on payday so the decision is already made before the temptation arrives. Remove easy instant access to your savings accounts so they require deliberate effort to reach. Create hard spending limits on your cards. Unsubscribe from the sales emails and shopping apps that are designed specifically to make you spend money you had not budgeted for.

Make your future self a financial priority before temporary desires take over. Because if you don't pay yourself first, your impulses and the entire retail marketing industry will gladly spend every cent for you.

3. Stay Away from Destructive Debt

Not all debt is bad, but careless debt can delay financial freedom for years.

High-interest consumer debt, unnecessary loans, and financing lifestyles you cannot truly afford can quietly drain your future income.

Debt should ideally be used strategically for assets that generate value—not liabilities that lose value.

Debt can be dangerous because it often allows people to appear financially successful long before the bill arrives.

I remember working with a woman named Debbie who seemed to be living what many people would consider a dream lifestyle.

Every single year, she and her husband took multiple trips to the Caribbean with their children, sometimes four vacations a year. From the outside, it looked glamorous. She always seemed to be traveling, enjoying life, and creating expensive experiences for her family.

I remember wondering how she could afford it all.

Later, I realized the lifestyle wasn't being funded by wealth, it was being funded by debt.

She had taken multiple loans to finance these trips and other expenses. Eventually, the debt became so severe that even her salary could no longer sustain her household obligations.

What looked like financial freedom was just financial pressure hidden behind vacation photos and temporary experiences.

That experience taught me an important lesson:

Just because someone looks wealthy does not mean they are financially secure.

Some people are financing lifestyles they cannot truly afford to impress other people online. This is called the "fake reel life" or FRL, for short.

Some people are one emergency away from financial collapse.

And some people are using debt to create an image that their income cannot support.

This doesn't mean you should never enjoy your money or create beautiful memories with your family.

It means learning to delay gratification.

Many financial mistakes happen because people want immediate rewards.

They want the vacation now.
The car now.
The apartment now.
The lifestyle now.

But wealth often requires sacrificing temporary comfort for long-term freedom.

Delayed gratification is one of the strongest predictors of financial discipline.

Your lifestyle should be built on cash flow, savings, and real financial stability, not borrowed money used to impress others.

Freedom feels very different when your memories are not attached to monthly repayments.

In our financial system, your credit score is essentially a financial passport. You don't need to lose money to invest in it, but you do need to understand how the system grades you. Think of credit not as a license to spend money you don't have, but as a tool to prove you are reliable.

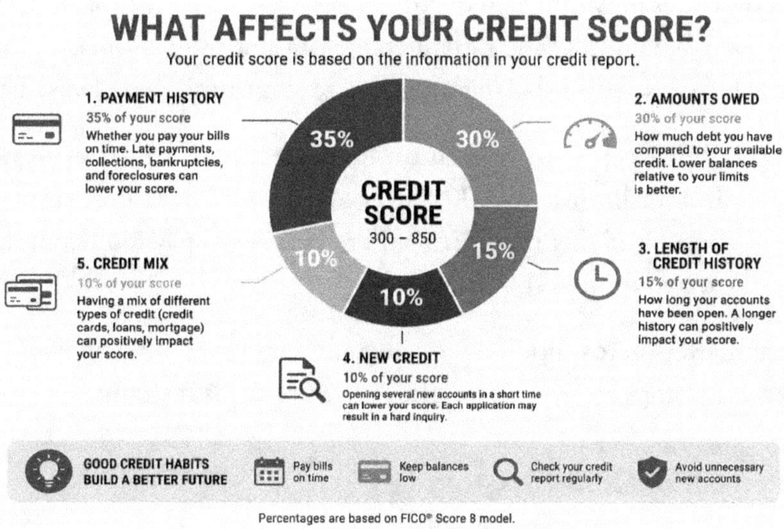

A standard FICO Score is calculated based on your creditworthiness, which relies on five distinct pillars:

1. Payment History (35%)

This is the single heaviest factor in your score. The system wants to know one thing: do you pay your bills exactly when they are due? Late payments, collections, or defaults will aggressively drag this number down.

- **Tip:** Put a small, recurring fixed bill (like a utility or streaming subscription) on a credit card, set the card to auto-pay the full statement balance every single month, and put the card away. You prove reliability without spending an extra dime.

This works because consistency is what the system is measuring, not complexity. One perfectly managed account is often stronger than several mismanaged ones.

2.. Amounts Owed / Credit Utilization (30%)

This measures how much credit you are actively using compared to your total available limit. Using too much of your limit signals financial stress to the bureaus. Lower balances relative to your limits are always better.

- **Tip:** Keep your utilization low (ideally under 10% to 30%). If your limit is $1,000, never let the statement post showing a balance higher than $300 and remember to pay it off completely to avoid interest.

What matters here is not how much credit you have, but how controlled your usage appears over time. The system rewards restraint.

3. Length of Credit History (15%)

The credit system rewards longevity. It tracks how long your accounts have been open and active. A longer history gives lenders a larger track record to trust.

- **Tip:** Keep your oldest accounts open. Even if you don't use your first credit card often, keeping it open and dormant (or with one tiny annual charge) anchors the age of your credit profile.

Closing old accounts can erase years of stability from your profile in an instant, which is why patience matters more than activity here.

4. New Credit (10%)

Opening multiple new credit lines or applying for several loans in a short window signals urgency and risk. Each formal application triggers a "hard inquiry," which can temporarily lower your score.

- **Tip:** Only apply for credit when it is necessary. Avoid the temptation of retail store card discounts at checkout lines; those unnecessary new accounts do more harm than good.

Every new application is essentially a signal to the system about your financial behavior under pressure.

5. Credit Mix (10%)

The system likes to see that you can responsibly manage different types of accounts over time—such as revolving credit (credit cards) and installment loans (mortgages or student loans).

- **Tip:** Do not take out loans just to "build a mix." Over time, as you naturally hit milestones like buying a home, this mix will diversify on its own.

This is one of the most misunderstood parts of credit scoring. Forced diversity is not rewarded; natural financial progression is.

The #1 Rule of Credit: Treat a credit card exactly like a debit card. If the cash isn't sitting in your checking account right now to pay for it, do not buy it. Use the system to build your score but never let the system take a penny of your wealth in interest.

4. Keep Your Wins Private

Not every financial milestone needs an audience.

Sometimes silence is strategy.

Moving quietly protects you from unnecessary pressure, comparison, jealousy, and people who suddenly feel entitled to your success.

There is power in building privately and announcing results later—or not at all.

In a world where people feel pressured to announce every achievement online, there is real power in learning how to build quietly.

During my twenties, life felt incredibly unstable.

I was moving between apartments.
Changing jobs.
Trying to figure out where I wanted to live.
And at times, I didn't even know what country I would
eventually settle in.

Because so much of my life felt uncertain, I found myself spending a lot of time in isolation.

At the time, that season felt incredibly lonely.

There were moments when I questioned whether I was falling behind because my life didn't look as polished or publicly celebrated as other people's lives seemed to appear.

But looking back, that solitude became one of the greatest gifts of my financial and personal journey.

It gave me space to truly learn about myself.

I spent time focusing on personal development.
I learned discipline.
I clarified what I wanted my future to look like.
I made financial decisions without outside noise.
And perhaps most importantly, I was protected from unnecessary

opinions, judgment, and pressure from people who did not understand my long-term goals.

Not everyone deserves access to your dreams while they are still developing.

Sometimes sharing too early invites doubt, criticism, comparison, or expectations that can distract you from your path.

Privacy can be a form of protection.

Silence can be a strategy.

And solitude, while uncomfortable, can sometimes become the environment where your greatest transformation happens.

Not every win needs an audience.

Some of your most important seasons will happen quietly—and that is perfectly okay.

5. Avoid Status Symbols and Flashy Labels

Many people spend money trying to *look* wealthy instead of becoming wealthy.

Luxury labels, expensive cars, designer items, and constant upgrades can become distractions if they are funded by insecurity rather than true financial stability.

Real wealth is ownership, cash flow and options.

Not logos.

Luxury cars, designer labels, expensive watches, and constant lifestyle upgrades can create the image of success while quietly delaying real financial freedom.

There's often truth behind the idea that people with real wealth do not always feel the need to loudly display it.

Mark Zuckerberg became one of the wealthiest men in the world while also becoming known for wearing simple grey t-shirts and, for a time, driving practical cars such as a Toyota Prius.

Warren Buffett still lives in the same home he purchased decades ago in Omaha, Nebraska despite being able to live almost anywhere in the world.

Caroline Kennedy is often associated with a more understated form of generational wealth—where status is less about logos and more about legacy, education, privacy, and long-term influence.

The bigger issue with status spending goes back to the first chapter topic of opportunity cost.

Every time you overspend trying to appear successful, you may be delaying investments that could build real wealth.

That designer bag could have gone toward your emergency fund. That luxury car payment could have gone toward your business. That constant lifestyle upgrading could have funded real estate, stocks, retirement savings, or future opportunities.

When building wealth, it helps to prioritize the four forms of wealth that matter most:

Financial wealth — money, investments, assets, ownership, and cash flow.

Time wealth — having control over your schedule and freedom over how you spend your life.

Health wealth — protecting your physical and mental well-being so you can enjoy your success.

Relationship wealth — building strong family relationships, friendships, networks, and communities that enrich your life.

Many people sacrifice all four to maintain an image.

They lose financial wealth through overspending.
They lose time wealth by working endlessly to sustain appearances.
They lose health wealth through stress.
And sometimes they lose relationship wealth through comparison, competition, or living beyond their means.

Real wealth is not about looking rich to strangers.

It's about building a life that is rich in options, peace, ownership, health, and meaningful relationships.

6. Understand Taxes

Many people focus on making money but know very little about keeping it.

Making money is one skill. Keeping money is another.

As your income grows, tax literacy stops being optional and becomes one of the most important financial skills you can develop. Taxes quietly shape every stage of financial life: your salary, your investments, your business profits, your property income, and your retirement planning. Two people can earn the exact same income and end up with very different levels of wealth depending entirely on how well they manage their tax obligations.

Understanding how taxes work is not about avoidance. It is about being intentional, organized, and strategic with money you have already earned.

In the US, the tax system is progressive, meaning you are taxed in layers. As your income increases, only the portion of income within each bracket is taxed at the higher rate, not your entire income. The mistake many people make is assuming that earning more means losing most of it to taxes. In reality, higher income still results in higher take-home pay, but only if you understand how the brackets work rather than being caught off guard by a tax bill you did not plan for.

As income grows, avoidable mistakes become more expensive. Not tracking deductible expenses properly. Mixing personal and business finances. Ignoring filing deadlines. Not understanding which income is taxable and which is not. Underestimating what you owe and getting hit with unexpected liabilities. And perhaps most commonly, increasing spending as income rises without accounting for the fact that a larger income also means a larger tax obligation.

One of the most powerful wealth-building tools available in the US is learning to use tax-advantaged accounts and legal structures that reduce your tax burden legally over time. Retirement accounts like a 401K or IRA offer tax-deferred or tax-free growth depending on which type you choose. Health Savings Accounts offer triple tax advantages for those who qualify. Business structures like an LLC or S-Corp can allow you to deduct legitimate business expenses that reduce your taxable income. And investment strategies like tax-loss harvesting can be used to offset gains in years when your portfolio has mixed results.

The principle underneath all of this is simple. It is not just about how much you earn. It is about how efficiently your money grows after tax. Long-term wealth is not built by earning more alone. It is built by keeping more, legally and intelligently, over time.

7. Invest in Yourself Before Anyone Else Does

There is a habit that sits quietly underneath every other habit in this chapter, and it is the one most people skip because it does not feel like a financial decision.

It is.

Investing in yourself, your skills, your knowledge, your health, and your ability to earn, is the foundation that every other wealth-building strategy rests on. You cannot out-invest a shrinking income. You cannot compound your way out of a career that has stopped growing. And you cannot build the kind of long-term financial independence this book is about if the person at the center of that plan is running on empty.

I learned this the hard way during a stretch of my career when I was so focused on saving and investing my income that I had stopped paying attention to the income itself. I was disciplined with my money but I had stopped being disciplined about my growth. And slowly, quietly, the gap between where I was and where I wanted to be stopped closing.

What changed things was a deliberate decision to invest in myself with the same seriousness I brought to everything else. A course that deepened a skill I was already being paid for. A coach who helped me see blind spots I had been too close to notice. Books that expanded how I thought about money, business, and my own potential. These were not luxuries. They were assets, and they generated returns the way assets do, compounding over time in ways that showed up in my earning power, my confidence, and the opportunities that started finding their way to me.

The women who build lasting wealth are almost always women who kept growing. They did not stop learning when they left school. They did not stop developing when they got the job. They understood that their ability to earn is itself an asset, and like any asset it requires maintenance, attention, and periodic reinvestment.

Your health belongs in this conversation too. This is not about aesthetics. It is about capacity. Your physical and mental wellbeing determines how consistently you can show up, how clearly you can think, and how long you can sustain the kind of focused effort that building real wealth requires. Neglecting your health to build your portfolio is a trade that tends to cost far more than it saves.

The quiet habit here is simple. Set aside a portion of your income, even a small percentage, specifically for your own growth. A course, a certification, a book, a therapist, a gym membership, a mentor. Treat it as a non-negotiable line item in your budget the same way you treat your savings contribution. Because the return on investing in yourself is the one return that no market correction can touch.

8. Learn to Say No

One of the most underestimated skills in building sustainable wealth is the ability to say no—firmly, consistently, and entirely without guilt. Every single financial "yes" you give carries a hidden cost. Many people remain stuck in place not because their income is too low, but because they repeatedly say yes to the wrong things.

Not every financial opportunity is a good one. Bad investments are rarely obvious at first; they usually arrive wrapped in a sense of urgency, intense hype, or emotional manipulation. Developing a quiet wealth mindset means resisting the pressure to deploy your money into things you do not fully understand, cannot easily explain to a child, or cannot afford to lose. True wealth builders prioritize the protection of their capital before they ever focus on growing it.

A significant portion of your financial decisions aren't financial at all—they are deeply social. People routinely overspend just to match their peer group, upgrade their lifestyles to avoid feeling left out, and make critical choices based on comparison rather than a clear strategy. Financial freedom requires you to accept a simple truth: just because a behavior is socially normal does not mean it is financially smart. Saying no to social expectations is often the exact line that separates absolute stability from chronic financial stress.

An incredibly vital, yet painful, boundary to establish is refusing to carry everyone else's financial burdens. As your success becomes visible, people, whether they are family, friends, or acquaintances, may begin to expect your support. While generosity is highly valuable, unchecked financial rescue behavior will quietly dismantle your own progress. Saying no does not mean you do not care. It means you recognize that you cannot pour from an empty cup. You can offer emotional, mental, or strategic support to the people you love without becoming their perpetual financial safety net.

Even if an opportunity offers a paycheck, it doesn't mean it deserves your time. Some projects are nothing more than high-paying distractions that pull you away from your long-term direction, drain your energy, or fail to build actual skills and assets.

Building wealth requires radical focus. If an opportunity does not explicitly align with your personal strategy, your core values, or your long-term plan, you must decline it, even if those around you don't understand the decision.

Saying no is not about limiting your life; it is about protecting it. It is the ultimate defense mechanism for your capital, your time, your focus, and your future. Ultimately, financial independence is shaped far less by the opportunities you accept, and far more by the ones you choose to refuse.

Wealth is often built quietly before it becomes visible publicly.

The habits that seem small today may be the exact habits that create extraordinary freedom tomorrow.

6

A Corporate girl's manual to the 401K and retirement savings

"Money trees is the perfect place for shade and that's just how I feel"

— KENDRICK LAMAR

We've all been there—the frantic, exhausting whirlwind of starting a new job. Picture this: it's your first week at work.

Day One

You walk into a bright, airy lobby and inform security that it's your first day. They hand you a company badge and, quite possibly, a handbook filled with policies, procedures, and building regulations that you'll probably never read again after today.

Soon, you're greeted by an HR representative or your manager, who escorts you to your desk. You put your belongings down and begin what should be a straightforward process: setting up your computer.

You enter your login credentials.

They don't work.

Your manager mentions she has a meeting and disappears before the issue can be resolved, so you turn to the person sitting nearest to you. Unfortunately, they have no idea how to help. They've worked at the company for fifteen years and can barely remember what their own onboarding process looked like. Still, they kindly provide you with the contact information for someone in IT.

After reaching out, you discover that IT hasn't even entered you into the system yet.

And so begins your first day.

You spend hours staring at a computer screen, occasionally clicking around and pretending to be productive while waiting for someone, somewhere, to grant you access to the tools required to do your job.

Around lunchtime, your manager returns and asks whether you'd like to join her for lunch.

A difficult decision, considering you've spent the entire morning doing absolutely nothing.

She explains that she'd like to introduce you to some of the people you'll be working with and give you a quick tour of the floor. As you make your way around, everyone seems remarkably cheerful. Colleagues greet each other warmly, conversations flow effortlessly, and the atmosphere appears almost too good to be true.

Three months later, you'll discover that most of these people barely speak to one another and spend much of their time avoiding each other in the hallway.

After lunch, you return to your desk and spend the rest of the day reading company policies, procedures, and fire evacuation protocols because, quite frankly, you have nothing else to do.

Day Two

The morning is consumed by technical setup.

You work with IT, follow installation instructions, reset passwords, and attempt to gain access to the various systems required for your role.

At 9:00 a.m., you're invited to your first team meeting.

Everyone around the table seems fluent in a language you've never heard before. Acronyms fly across the room at lightning speed. Projects, systems, and processes are referenced as though everyone was born knowing what they mean.

To be fair, you've been hired because of your knowledge and expertise, so much of the terminology sounds familiar. Still, you're not entirely sure whether contributing this early would make you seem engaged or simply overly eager.

So, you choose the safest option available.

You smile.

You nod.

And you spend the entire meeting pretending you know exactly what's going on.

Later that day, your manager provides you with an onboarding checklist and asks you to review it. She also mentions that she has a useful document containing all the company's common acronyms and their meanings.

"It really helped me when I started," she says.

She offers to send it to you.

She never does.

Eventually, you create your own glossary, adding new entries every time someone casually drops another mysterious abbreviation into a conversation.

Day Three

By the afternoon, an email arrives from HR containing information about your employee benefits.

The document is extensive.

It outlines health and dental insurance plans, coverage levels, deductibles, out-of-pocket maximums, in-network versus out-of-network costs, and a variety of optional enhancements.

There are also sections covering life insurance, disability insurance, wellness programs, and additional benefit packages.

Then comes the retirement information.

Pages of explanations detail 401(k) plans, employer matching contributions, vesting schedules, investment options, and a collection of financial terminology that may as well be written in another language.

You understand the importance of health and dental insurance. Those seem straightforward enough.

Everything else appears optional.

Why?

Because nobody has discussed any of it with you.

The company mentions that educational workshops are available to explain the various benefits and answer questions. However, like most new employees, you're busy trying to learn your job, understand company systems, remember people's names, and figure out where the nearest coffee machine is located.

Attending a retirement planning seminar feels like a problem for a future version of yourself.

But had you attended one of those 401(k) and retirement planning sessions, you would have discovered that some of the most important financial decisions of your career were hidden within those seemingly optional benefits packages.

Here's what would have been discussed.

Firstly, the name 401(k), literally originates from the U.S. tax code. Section 401 (k) of the Internal Revenue Code refers to a retirement savings plan where employees are allowed to defer a portion of their salary before any taxes are taken out. In essence, because it is offered through your employer, you can contribute part of your salary into the account, and it grows over time through investment. The advantage of the 401(k) is that because the contributions are pre-tax, it lowers your taxable income now and you pay taxes later when you withdraw in retirement.

As you continue reviewing your retirement options, you'll likely come across two additional accounts that often appear in retirement planning discussions: the Traditional IRA and the Roth IRA.

At first glance, they seem nearly identical. Both are designed to help you save for retirement, both offer tax advantages, and both allow your investments to grow over time. The key difference lies in *when* you pay taxes.

Traditional IRA and a Roth IRA are both tax-advantaged retirement accounts—but they flip *when* you pay taxes. That timing difference ends up driving everything else.

The core difference

- **Traditional IRA** → tax break *now*, taxes *later*
- **Roth IRA** → taxes *now*, tax-free *later*

Category	Traditional 401k / IRA	Roth IRA
Benefits	Upfront tax deduction for contributions	No upfront tax deduction for contributions
Tax	Retirement withdrawals are fully taxed	Tax-free retirement withdrawals
Penalties	Pre-retirement withdrawals are taxed and could be charged a 10% penalty	Allows early withdrawals of contributions; only investment gains are taxed and penalized
RMDs	Required minimum distributions start at age 73	No required minimum distributions

The Traditional IRA

A Traditional IRA rewards you today.

Contributions may reduce your taxable income in the year you make them, which can lower your current tax bill. Once the money is invested, it grows tax-deferred, meaning you won't owe taxes on investment gains each year.

The tradeoff comes later.

When you withdraw money in retirement, those withdrawals are generally taxed as ordinary income.

In simple terms, a Traditional IRA follows this formula:

Tax break now. Taxes later.

This option can be attractive if you believe you'll be in a lower tax bracket during retirement than you are today.

Most people dismiss retirement accounts because they feel distant.

But they are not distant decisions.

They are early financial "settings" that quietly determine how your money behaves for decades.

Two people can earn the same salary and still end up in completely different financial positions later in life, not because one earned more, but because one understood how to structure what they already earned.

The Roth IRA

A Roth IRA works in the opposite direction.

Contributions are made with money that has already been taxed. You don't receive an immediate tax deduction, but your investments grow tax-free, and qualified withdrawals in retirement are completely tax-free.

The formula is simple:

Taxes now. Tax-free later.

This can be especially appealing if you expect your income—and potentially your tax rate—to be higher in the future. It also provides certainty in a world where future tax rates remain unknown.

Both accounts benefit from one of the most powerful forces in personal finance: compound growth.

The longer your money remains invested, the more opportunity it has to generate returns, which then generate their own returns. Over long periods of time, this compounding effect can become far more powerful than the original amount you contributed.

The Roth IRA has a unique advantage in this regard.

Because qualified withdrawals are tax-free, all that compounded growth belongs to you. None of it is taxed when you retire.

If you begin investing in your mid-twenties, a significant portion of your retirement balance may ultimately come from investment growth rather than your original contributions. The larger that growth becomes, the more valuable the Roth's tax-free treatment can be.

Another important difference involves access to your money.

With a Roth IRA, you can generally withdraw your original contributions at any time without taxes or penalties. While this shouldn't be viewed as a substitute for an emergency fund, it does provide an additional layer of flexibility.

The investment earnings, however, typically remain protected until retirement unless certain exceptions apply.

Traditional IRAs are less forgiving. Early withdrawals are generally subject to both income taxes and penalties, making them less flexible for unexpected financial needs.

Roth IRAs have income limits. As your income increases, your ability to contribute directly may be reduced or eliminated altogether.

Traditional IRAs do not have income limits for making contributions. However, your ability to deduct those contributions may be limited if you earn above certain thresholds or participate in an employer-sponsored retirement plan.

For many people, eligibility rules become an important factor when deciding which account to use.

Traditional IRAs come with another consideration.

At a certain age, the government requires you to begin taking withdrawals, known as Required Minimum Distributions (RMDs). These withdrawals ensure that the deferred taxes are eventually collected.

Roth IRAs do not require withdrawals during your lifetime.

This gives Roth accounts additional flexibility for long-term planning and can make them useful tools for leaving assets to heirs. It also means you have greater control over when and how your retirement assets are used.

If you're early in your career, perhaps in your twenties or early thirties, your income today may be lower than it will be later in life.

In that situation, paying taxes now and allowing decades of tax-free growth through a Roth IRA often makes sense.

If you're in your peak earning years and facing a higher tax burden today, the immediate tax deduction provided by a Traditional IRA may be more valuable.

At its core, the decision comes down to a simple question:

When would you rather pay taxes?

A Traditional IRA says: "I believe I'll pay less tax later than I would today, "A Roth IRA says: "I'm willing to pay taxes today so I can avoid them later."

Neither approach is universally right or wrong. In many ways, you're making an educated guess about your future income, future tax rates, and future financial circumstances.

For many young professionals, the Roth IRA is often the simpler and more attractive option. It offers tax-free growth, tax-free retirement withdrawals, greater flexibility, and no required withdrawals during your lifetime.

The Traditional IRA remains a valuable tool, particularly for individuals in higher tax brackets who want to reduce their taxable income today.

The most important lesson, however, is that choosing between a Traditional IRA and a Roth IRA is far less important than failing to invest at all.

The account you start today will almost always outperform the perfect account you plan to open someday.

Many people eventually use *both* to diversify their tax exposure.

The biggest advantage for a new hire is that companies tend to offer the ability to match a portion of your contributions. Assuming you have a $100,000 salary, you opt for a 3% match, and an average return of 10%, you'd have $1,030,950 in your 401(k) in about 20 years.

This is essentially free money: if you don't contribute, all the money the company is offering to match will be left on the table.

Something important that many people don't consider when they first start contributing to their 401(k) is the company's vesting schedule. Many employees assume that every dollar shown in their retirement account automatically belongs to them. However, employer contributions often come with conditions attached, making it important to understand exactly when those funds become yours fully.

Vesting refers to how much of your employer's contributions you own, assuming you were to leave the company. A lot of companies require you to stay for a certain number of years before you fully own the match. This was an issue when I had to leave my first corporate role. I had assumed that if I were to quit my job, I would take all the money, including the match, with me.

However, the company had a Cliff Vesting schedule in place, which meant I owned 0% until I hit 3 years, at which point I would have been able to own all the money in my 401(k). So, I was only entitled to the portion I had contributed to the plan.

Other vesting schedules are graded, so ownership increases a little each year. For example, 30% after 1 year, 40% after 2 years, 50% after 3 years. This way, if you leave after a certain period, you will always be eligible for a portion of the match.

If your company offers a match (e.g., they match 3–5% of your salary), that's essentially extra compensation. Not contributing enough to secure the full match leaves money on the table.

A retirement account isn't just a savings account; you usually need to choose investments. Many plans default to target-date funds, which automatically adjust risk over time. Otherwise, broad index funds are a simple, effective choice. If you are younger, you can afford market ups and downs.

Historically, equities have outperformed safer assets over long periods, so being overly conservative early can hurt your growth. Pulling money out early often leads to penalties and lost long-term gains. Treat this money as "locked away for the future you."

Another good rule is to increase your contribution percentage whenever your salary increases. Aim for approximately 10–15% of income over time (including employer match).

When you change jobs, you can usually roll your retirement account into a new plan or a personal account. Don't cash it out. Some people have criticized the 401 (k) plans for 1) having extremely high fees and 2) not performing as well as expected, but as long as you are getting the company match, it's always going to be free money since employers offering a matching contribution, which is really just a part of your salary and not subject to income tax.

401K Company Match WITHOUT factoring growth potential

Your Salary	4% Match	5% Match	6% Match
$50,000	$60,000	$75,000	$90,000
$60,000	$72,000	$90,000	$108,000
$70,000	$84,000	$105,000	$126,000
$80,000	$96,000	120,000	$144,000
$90,000	$108,000	$135,000	$162,000
$100,000	$120,000	$150,000	$180,000
$200,000	$240,000	$300,000	$360,000
$300,000	$360,000	$450,000	$540,000
$400,000	$480,000	$600,000	$720,000
$500,000	$600,000	$750,000	$900,000

A person earning $100,000 per year at a company offering a 5% match could receive approximately $150,000 in employer contributions over their career. Someone earning $200,000 with the same match could receive $300,000.

And that's before a single dollar of investment growth is considered.

This is why financial professionals often describe the employer match as an immediate return on your money. If your company matches your contribution, you're effectively receiving additional compensation simply for participating in the plan.

The reality is even more powerful than the numbers shown above. In the real world, those employer contributions are typically invested. Over decades, the combination of employer contributions and compound growth can transform what appears to be a modest annual benefit into a substantial retirement asset.

In other words, the employer match isn't just free money, it's free money with decades to grow.

7

Salaried Employee vs. Starting your own business

"Working 9-5, what a way to make a livin'/Barely getting' by/It's all taking and no givin'"

— DOLLY PARTON

At 25, she worked in a glass building in Midtown Manhattan that looked far more glamorous from the outside than it felt on the inside.

She had just gotten the job after two years of internships, entry-level rejections, and dozens of applications that disappeared into the silence of automated hiring systems. When the offer letter finally came, her family celebrated like she had made it.

Her starting salary was $58,000 a year. To her parents and the extended family members who compared her to cousins still searching for work, this was proof that she was successful.

To her? It felt like relief.

She moved into a small one-bedroom apartment in Brooklyn because she was tired of long commutes and wanted her own space.

Her monthly expenses told a different story than her salary suggested. Rent cost $1,600 a month. Transportation on the subway and the occasional Uber added another $150. Food, between groceries and the takeout she ordered on the nights she was too tired to cook, ran close to $500. She sent money home to her family every month, $200 that felt both necessary and quietly draining. Subscriptions, phone bill, skincare, and the professional appearance that corporate life quietly demanded accounted for another $300. Emergency expenses were unpredictable. What was left over at the end of the month rarely matched what she had imagined when she first saw that offer letter.

She realized quickly that a good salary in New York City could feel very average once real life entered the chat.

Her day started at 5:00 a.m.

She woke up exhausted because she had fallen asleep around 1 a.m. finishing work that her manager had labeled urgent.

She got dressed carefully because appearance mattered. Looking too casual could be read as unserious. Looking too polished could draw the wrong kind of attention.

By 6:15 a.m. she was on the subway, mentally rehearsing the day ahead while the city moved around her, or she was negotiating with a rideshare app that kept surging its prices, or she was standing on a platform praying the train was not delayed again. She arrived at the office before her official start time not because anyone had asked her to, but because she had learned quickly that the people who arrived on time were the same people who got quietly noticed for the wrong reasons.

She got to work around 8 a.m. but her official start time was 9.

Nobody explicitly told employees to arrive early.

They just quietly noticed who didn't.

Her manager, a man in his late 40s, constantly called her "young lady."

Not her name.

"Young lady."

"Young lady, fix this deck."

"Young lady, stay back after work."

"Young lady, why are you in a hurry to go home?"

He praised her publicly but privately overloaded her with work because she was efficient.

Her coworkers weren't always easier.

One female colleague treated mentorship like competition.

Another colleague regularly disappeared during difficult projects but reappeared during presentations to speak the loudest.

A male coworker once told her:

"You're lucky you're pretty. Things come easier for women like you."

She smiled politely while silently calculating prison sentences.

At 25, she also became an unofficial family investment fund.

Her younger sibling needed school fees.

An aunt needed help with hospital bills.

A cousin wanted business capital.

When she said no, some relatives called her selfish because they saw her corporate lifestyle online and assumed wealth.

They didn't see her Excel budgeting sheet.

They saw brunch photos.

Then came layoffs.

Her company announced restructuring.

Suddenly everyone who had been posting motivational quotes on LinkedIn became terrified.

People started over-performing.

Managers became colder.

Coworkers withheld information.

Rumors spread daily.

Who would be cut?

Would she survive?

For three months she lived in anxiety.

She stopped sleeping properly.

She developed stress acne.

Her chest tightened every time HR sent calendar invites.

One Friday afternoon, she watched a respected senior employee escorted out after 11 years at the company.

No warning.

No graceful goodbye.

Just gone.

That broke something in her.

She realized loyalty was often one-directional.

The company expected sacrifice.

But would replace people by Monday.

That night in her apartment, she opened her laptop and began researching alternatives.

She investigated real estate investing in more affordable markets outside of New York. She studied short-term rental models and how people were building income through platforms like Airbnb. She researched digital consulting, freelancing, and passive income streams that did not require her physical presence to generate revenue. She took notes on everything. She started waking up earlier so she could work on herself before work consumed her.

Six months later she had savings. A side business. Investment knowledge. An emergency funds.

Most importantly?

Options.

Then something ironic happened.

Once she no longer desperately needed the job emotionally, she performed better. She became more assertive. She negotiated her compensation. She stopped seeking approval she had not asked for. She took her annual leave without guilt. She left the office at a reasonable hour when the work was done.

She understood that employment could be useful, but dangerous if it became your only identity.

She learned that being salaried can teach you structure, discipline, and professionalism.

But if you're not intentional about it, a salary can quietly train you to confuse comfort with security.

And those are very different things.

At 25, she had what looked like stability on paper.

A corporate job in Manhattan. A direct deposit that made family members say, "You're doing well." Business casual outfits, Friday team lunches, and LinkedIn posts about professional growth. The polished surface of someone who had arrived.

But her boss called her "brilliant" in meetings and messaged her at 11:47 p.m. asking for a revised deck marked urgent. She learned office politics quickly. The coworker who smiled warmly and consistently took credit for her ideas. The manager who described young women as "aggressive" the moment they tried to negotiate their pay. The HR department that held seminars about work-life balance while quietly rewarding burnout. The subtle unspoken pressure to always appear polished, pleasant, and endlessly grateful for the opportunity.

Her salary hit her account and disappeared with alarming speed. Rent. Family support. Transport. A friend's wedding contribution. Skincare because you have to look presentable. Emergency expenses she had not planned for. By the eighteenth of every month she would stare at her banking app wondering how it was possible to work this hard and still feel financially fragile.

Then there was the emotional contradiction that nobody had warned her about. At family gatherings the question was always "When are you getting married?" At work the question was "Are you sure you can handle this level of responsibility?" She was simultaneously too young to be taken seriously and old enough to have everything figured out.

Some nights she cried from exhaustion because adulthood felt like performing competence while quietly panicking on the inside.

Other nights she felt powerful. Like the first time she paid her own rent. The first time she bought her mother something expensive. The first time she turned down a disrespectful job offer because she knew her value.

She began noticing something important. The salary was giving her survival, but not freedom. She watched colleagues in their 40s who were still trapped, waiting on promotions, terrified of layoffs, living above their means to maintain an appearance of success that had stopped feeling worth the cost.

And she asked herself a dangerous question.

"If this job disappeared tomorrow, who am I outside of this paycheck?"

That question changed everything.

She started investing in broad-market index funds. She researched real estate in markets outside of New York where her money could go further. She began freelancing on weekends, building skills and income that belonged entirely to her and did not require anyone's permission to pursue.

She stopped seeing her salary as the destination.

It became seed capital. A training ground. A temporary chapter.

Being a salaried employee taught her discipline, professionalism, and resilience.

But the biggest lesson?

A paycheck can give you independence.

Only ownership gives you leverage.

She didn't start with a big idea. And she didn't quit her job to follow a passion.

Her life looked polished from the outside. A decent apartment in Hoboken, brunches with friends in the West Village, a curated Instagram presence, and the kind of professional trajectory that made people at family dinners say "she's doing really well." But behind the surface she was exhausted, her salary was disappearing faster than she could track it, and layoffs in the tech sector were making everyone in her office nervous.

Then she noticed something while apartment hunting for a friend who was relocating to the city from out of state.

Young professionals moving to New York were running into the same problems everywhere. Misleading listings. Unresponsive brokers. Outrageous broker fees. Short-term rentals that were overpriced and inconsistent. A complete lack of trustworthy guidance for people trying to navigate one of the most complicated rental markets in the country. And for Americans relocating from other cities or returning from abroad, the process was even more overwhelming.

She saw a problem people were desperate to solve. That became her business.

Phase 1: Start as a Service Business

She did not buy property. She could not afford that.

Instead, she started as a rental placement and relocation concierge, helping people navigate the New York City housing market without getting burned. She helped young professionals find verified, fairly priced apartments. She helped people relocating from other states or returning from abroad secure housing before they arrived. She helped landlords find vetted, reliable tenants. She helped short-term rental owners improve their occupancy and their reviews.

She spent her weekends visiting apartments in Brooklyn, Hoboken, Jersey City, and Astoria, building a personal database of verified listings and trustworthy contacts that no app could replicate.

She built a simple website, an Instagram presence, and a Google business profile. She registered her business as an LLC.

Startup costs were modest. Her phone was already owned. The website cost $800. Branding and photography ran $1,200. Transportation for property inspections over the first three months added up to about $600. Business registration and basic legal setup cost $500. Total startup investment was roughly $3,100.

She kept her job.

Phase 2: First Money

Her first client was a software engineer relocating from Austin to New York City. He paid a $1,500 relocation service fee. In exchange she handled apartment tours, lease negotiation support, furnishing recommendations, and utility setup guidance. That single transaction showed her something she had not fully understood before: service businesses can generate real cash quickly, without inventory, without a storefront, and without quitting your job to get started.

Within six months she was working with ten to fifteen clients a month. Monthly profit averaged $6,000 to $8,000. Her salary had become secondary.

Phase 3: Reinvest into Assets

Most people at this stage increase their lifestyle spending. She didn't.

Instead, she used her profits to lease a furnished one-bedroom apartment in Jersey City and convert it into a short-term rental listed on Airbnb and Furnished Finder. She did not own the property. She controlled a cash-flowing asset.

The lease cost $2,200 a month. Furniture and setup ran $4,500. Utilities, security deposits, and initial marketing brought the total startup investment to approximately $8,500.

The apartment generated between $3,500 and $6,000 a month depending on occupancy, which meant she recovered her setup costs within two months and was cash-flow positive before the end of the quarter.

Phase 4: Scale

By 28, she was managing multiple short-term rental units across the New York metro area. She had hired a cleaning crew, a part-time property coordinator, a photographer who handled all her listings, and a virtual assistant who managed guest communications.

She launched a premium relocation company specifically serving professionals moving to New York from other major US cities and Americans returning from postings abroad. She began partnering with boutique real estate agencies, earning referral commissions on lease signings and property sales for clients she connected to their listings.

Phase 5: Wealth Building

By 31, her income streams included relocation service fees, short-term rental profits, real estate referral commissions, and consulting work for other hosts and small property managers trying to optimize their operations.

She used those profits to purchase her first investment property, a two-bedroom condo in a market outside of New York where her capital went significantly further. Eventually she began building a small portfolio of income-producing properties in cities where strong rental demand met more accessible price points.

Her biggest lesson was simple.

She didn't begin with capital. She began with a service.

Service businesses create the fastest path for young people to build the capital that buys assets.

And assets create real wealth.

You will often hear that no one gets rich with a salary. I want to push back on that.

A salary, used wisely, is one of the most powerful wealth-building tools available to a young professional. It is stable, predictable income that arrives whether the market is up or down, whether your side business had a good month or a slow one, whether you are feeling motivated or running on fumes. That reliability is not a weakness. It is a foundation.

What the saying really means, and what her story illustrates, is that a salary alone is not enough. Relying on a salary as your only source of income and your only financial strategy is where the danger lives. Not in the salary itself, but in the trap of treating it as a destination rather than a starting point.

The women who build lasting wealth are rarely the ones who abandoned their careers in dramatic pursuit of something else. They are more often the ones who used their careers strategically. They learned their industries from the inside. They saved consistently. They invested early. They built something on the side while keeping their income secure. And at some point, sometimes gradually and sometimes all at once, the assets they had been quietly building began to generate more than the job ever had.

The salary was never the enemy. Staying only inside it was.

Use it as a runway, not a resting place. Use it as seed capital, not a ceiling. And build, quietly and consistently, toward the kind of ownership that no restructuring announcement on a Tuesday morning can take away from you.

8

Advisors you should know for Financial Success

"Promise me you gon'stack/Promise me you gon'ball
Promise me you'll invest three fourths of it all"

— ANDRE 3000

She was earning well in New York City, growing a business, and posting polished milestones online.

From the outside, people said she was ahead.

But privately, she kept running into expensive mistakes that had one root cause:

She had ambition. But no advisory team.

She realized that wealthy people often build a personal board of directors long before they become visibly wealthy. They do not wait until they have problems to find the right people. They build those relationships early, so that when the problems arrive, and they always do, the right voices are already in their corner.

Here is what each advisor does, and what it can cost you not to have them.

1) Lawyer: protects you from costly signatures

At 26, she was excited to lease her first commercial space in Manhattan.

The landlord rushed her.

"Other people are interested. If you don't sign today, you'll lose it."

She signed without legal review.

The lease had clauses she had not noticed. Sudden rent increase provisions. Maintenance costs shifted entirely to the tenant. Unclear exit terms. Financial penalties buried in the fine print.

She lost tens of thousands of dollars trying to exit that lease.

A good commercial lawyer reviews contracts before you sign them, not after the damage is done. They help with leases, business partnerships, trademark registration, employment agreements, and protecting the intellectual property you are building. A personal or family lawyer handles the other side of life, wills, trusts, and legal structures that protect what you own.

You should know one good commercial lawyer and one personal lawyer. When you are ready to formalize a business, registering as an LLC through your state's Secretary of State office is typically the first step, and a lawyer can walk you through what structure makes the most sense for your situation.

2) Accountant / Tax advisor: keeps success from becoming chaotic

As revenue grew fast, she celebrated the deposits, but she ignored structure.

Then tax notices started arriving.

She had mixed personal and business money in the same accounts. No accounting software. Incomplete records. No clear picture of what was profit versus what was just revenue moving through. What looked impressive from the outside was chaos on the inside.

A good accountant or tax advisor files your taxes properly, helps you avoid penalties that come from disorganization rather than dishonesty, structures your payroll correctly as you bring on staff, monitors your margins so you know where money is actually going, and prepares you for audits before they happen rather than scrambling during them.

Most importantly they help you separate your business and personal finances from the beginning, which is one of the most important habits you can build early. You can make money and still be completely financially disorganized. A good accountant makes sure those two things never happen at the same time.

3) Therapist: protects your mind from self-destruction

No one told her that unresolved emotional issues show up in financial decisions.

After burnout, she started impulse shopping. Not because she needed anything, but because buying things was the only thing that felt like control when everything else felt out of her hands.

After heartbreak, she overworked. She poured herself into her business not as strategy but as escape, logging eighteen-hour days not to build something but to avoid feeling something.

After professional rejection, she made emotional investments. She put money into opportunities she had not properly evaluated because she needed to feel like she was moving forward, like she was doing something, like she was still winning somewhere.

None of these were financial decisions. They were emotional ones wearing the clothes of financial decisions.

Therapy helped her see the patterns she could not see from inside them. The validation addiction that made her take on clients and projects she should have declined just to feel chosen. The burnout cycles she kept repeating because she had never learned to rest without guilt. The relationships she stayed in too long because leaving felt financially and emotionally too complicated to untangle. The fear-driven decision making that disguised itself as ambition.

A therapist is not a luxury. For anyone building something serious in a city that rewards performance and punishes vulnerability, protecting your mental clarity is as financially important as protecting your credit score.

You cannot build wealth while constantly emotionally collapsing. And you cannot see your financial blind spots clearly when the person doing the seeing is exhausted, unhealed, or running on anxiety and adrenaline alone.

Invest in your mind with the same seriousness you bring to your money. The return is real.

4) Financial planner / investment advisor: helps your wealth grow with direction

She followed social media investment hype. Someone promised to double her money quickly.

She lost heavily.

Then she found a real, fee-only financial advisor. Not someone earning commissions on the products they sold her. Someone whose incentive was aligned with her actual financial outcomes.

They walked her through building a proper emergency fund before touching any investment. They introduced her to index investing through broad market funds like the S&P 500. They helped her understand how to use her 401K and Roth IRA properly. They talked through diversification, what it means and what it doesn't. They introduced the concept of liquidity planning, making sure she always had accessible cash for the near term so she was never forced to sell long-term investments at the wrong time.

Wealth is not built through excitement. It is built through allocation.

And allocation requires a system, not opinions.

5) Insurance advisor: protects you from one unfortunate event

A friend got hospitalized unexpectedly.

Medical bills wiped out years of savings.

Another friend lost her entire product inventory in a warehouse fire with no financial backup.

Both situations had the same pattern: no insurance, no buffer, no recovery plan.

An insurance advisor helps you understand what coverage you need at each stage of your life. They advise on business, health, life and property insurance, as well as disability insurance and vehicle coverage. In the US, navigating health insurance options, whether through an employer, the ACA marketplace at healthcare.gov, or a private plan, can be genuinely confusing, and having someone walk you through the real differences in coverage, deductibles, and out-of-pocket maximums is worth every minute of that conversation.

One bad day should not erase a decade of progress.

That is the entire argument for insurance in a single sentence.

6) Career mentor: sharpens your choices

She worked hard in her corporate role. She delivered results. But her compensation did not always reflect her output.

A mentor changed that.

They taught her how to negotiate her salary with data rather than emotion. They coached her on executive presence, the way she communicated in meetings, the way she framed her contributions, the way she asked for things. They helped her recognize when a role had run its course and when staying was costing more than leaving. They showed her how to navigate office politics without compromising her integrity or her effectiveness. And they walked her through the practical mechanics of increasing her total compensation, not just her base salary but her bonus structure, her equity, her benefits, all of it.

Within a year her compensation jumped significantly.

Hard work matters, but without guidance, it is often underpriced.

7) Business mentor: saves you from first-timer mistakes

This is someone who has built, failed, scaled, and managed real systems.

Not social media motivation. Actual companies.

They have hired people, managed operations, dealt with suppliers, navigated the chaos of early growth, and figured out how to retain customers when the initial excitement wore off. They have made the expensive mistakes so you do not have to, and more importantly they can recognize when you are about to make one before you realize it yourself.

One conversation with the right person at the right time can save you from months of painful and expensive trial and error.

That is not an exaggeration. That is the compounding value of experience.

8) Banker: helps you access capital

Initially, she avoided debt completely. She associated it with risk.

Then she learned that strategic leverage, used correctly, is one of the tools that separates people who build wealth from people who only accumulate it slowly.

A strong banking relationship opens doors that a strong credit score alone cannot. Business checking and savings accounts structured properly from the beginning. Access to business lines of credit when cash flow needs a bridge. Equipment financing for purchases that would otherwise drain operating capital. And a banker who understands your business model and can advocate for you when you need it.

In the US, community banks and credit unions often offer more personalized service for small business owners than large national banks do. The Small Business Administration, commonly known as the SBA, also offers loan programs specifically designed for entrepreneurs who need capital but do not yet have the track record that traditional lenders require. Building a relationship with a banker before you need a loan makes the conversation significantly easier when the time comes.

9) Estate planner: protects what happens after you

Young people ignore this because death feels distant. But wealth without structure does not transfer smoothly.

If you own assets such as land, businesses, investments, or intellectual property, you need a will. You need to understand how trusts work and whether one makes sense for your situation. You need succession planning so that the assets you have spent years building, are passed on to the people you intend to receive them, and not to the state or to family members whose relationships with your estate you never got to define.

Many families lose generational wealth not because the wealth was poorly built, but because it was poorly protected. A will takes a few hours to draft with the right attorney. Not having one can cost your family years of legal complexity and significant financial loss.

This advisor is not for the future version of you that is older and wealthier. It is for the version of you that exists right now, building something worth protecting.

10) Spiritual advisor / wise elder: helps give you purpose and alignment

Success attracts noise, envy, pressure and comparison.

As your income grows and your visibility increases, so does the number of people with opinions about what you should do, who you should trust, which opportunity you should chase, and how you should be spending the life you are building.

A grounded spiritual advisor, whether that is a pastor, an imam, an elder, a therapist who works from a values-based framework, or simply a wise person whose life you deeply respect, helps you make decisions from a place of wisdom rather than ego or anxiety. They are the person you call when an opportunity feels right on paper but something in you is not sure. They are the voice that reminds you of your values when the noise gets loud.

Not every opportunity should be pursued.

Not every relationship deserves access.

Not every season requires acceleration.

Sometimes the most strategic decision is restraint.

Her biggest lesson? Most people think wealth is built through income alone. But often wealth is protected and expanded through: better advice, better systems, and better decisions.

And just as importantly, knowing who to call before things go wrong.

9

Designing your "soft" life

"No man could test me, impress me
My cash flow would never ever end..."

— GWEN STEFANI

What is all this money for? I remember sitting at my desk one evening, two years into a job that looked impressive on paper and felt hollow in practice, staring at a spreadsheet that showed I was technically on track. Savings rate: good. Investment contributions: consistent. Emergency fund: fully funded. Everything the books told me to do, I was doing.

And I felt nothing.

Not satisfied. Not free. Not even particularly motivated to keep going. Just tired in the way that comes from working very hard towards a goal you have stopped being sure you want.

I closed the laptop and sat with that feeling for a while. And the question that came up was not "how do I earn more" or "what should I invest in next." It was simpler and more unsettling than that.

What is all this money for?

It sounds like a simple question.

Yet many people spend years chasing financial goals without ever stopping to ask themselves.

Too many financial books focus almost exclusively on accumulation: save more, invest more, earn more, and retire rich.

Those things matter.

But *what kind of life are you actually trying to build?*

Money is a tool; its value comes from what it allows you to experience, protect, create, and enjoy.

Many women are not simply trying to become wealthy on paper. They are trying to create lives that feel peaceful, flexible, meaningful, and beautiful. They want financial security, but they also want freedom. They want options. They want the ability to make decisions based on what matters to them rather than what their bank account forces them to do.

That is where the idea of a "soft life" becomes important.

A soft life is not laziness.

It is not avoiding responsibility.

It is not spending money recklessly to create the appearance of luxury.

A truly soft life is one designed intentionally enough that nothing feels like a constant emergency.

It is a life in which money supports your well-being rather than constantly competing with it.

Defining wealth beyond money

Wealth doesn't have a universal definition.

What feels like success to one woman may feel completely unappealing to another.

For some women, wealth means building a highly successful career, leading large organizations, and creating influence through their work.

For others, wealth means flexibility. The ability to attend children's school events, care for aging parents, travel frequently, or work fewer hours without financial anxiety.

For others, it means creative freedom. The ability to write, build, teach, create, volunteer, or pursue meaningful work without worrying about whether every activity generates income.

For one woman, wealth may look like a penthouse overlooking a major city skyline.

For another, it may look like a quiet home near family, a garden, and having enough passive income to leave corporate life.

For another, it may simply mean never having to stay in a toxic relationship because she lacks financial options.

The point is not choosing the "right" version of wealth, but defining your version before society defines it for you.

Because if you never decide what "enough" looks like, "enough" will never arrive.

Time is the ultimate luxury

Ask any high earner who is also deeply exhausted whether they feel wealthy and watch what happens to their face.

The money is there. The account balance confirms it. But can they attend their child's school event without rescheduling three meetings first? Can they care for aging parents without their income dropping? Can they rest, genuinely rest, without a low-level financial anxiety humming underneath everything? Can they book a flight on a Wednesday morning without calculating what it will cost them in lost productivity?

For a lot of financially successful women the answer to most of those questions is no. And if the answer is no, then something important is missing from the picture regardless of what the bank account says.

Money without time control can feel like another trap. A more comfortable trap, certainly. A trap with better furniture and a nicer zip code. But a trap nonetheless.

True financial freedom is not just earning a high salary, having a nice home, or being able to afford vacations. It is the ability to step away from your physical location while your income continues to flow. It is being able to say "I'm going to Paris for two weeks" or "I need to be with my family right now" or "I need space to think" and having nothing collapse financially while you are gone.

That requires something most financial education does not teach directly. It requires income that is decoupled from your time.

Many people who appear financially successful are location-bound earners. If they stop working, the money stops. If they travel, their productivity drops and with it their income. If they rest, they pay for it financially. They are earning well but they are still tied, still hostage to their own hours in a way that looks like freedom from the outside but does not feel like it from the inside.

Real freedom looks different. It looks like businesses that run without your daily presence. Investments that generate returns whether you are paying attention or not. Systems, teams, and automations that continue producing value while you live your life. This is the shift from income to ownership that has been threading through every chapter of this book.

Here is what supports that kind of freedom structurally. Ownership income from businesses, equity stakes, dividends, and royalties. Investment income from stocks, index funds, real estate, and private investments. And systems-based income from teams, automations, digital products, and scalable services that do not require you to personally show up for every transaction.

There is a hidden contradiction that many women experience and rarely name out loud. They have been told their whole lives to be independent, to be successful, to earn their own money. But they were not always taught how to make that money non-dependent on their constant presence. So they end up earning well but unable to rest. Unable to fully pause. Unable to step away during motherhood, or grief, or illness, or any of the seasons of life that require a woman to be somewhere other than her desk.

That is not a soft life. That is structured dependency on labor wearing the costume of success.

The deeper shift happens when the question changes. It stops being "how much do I earn?" and becomes "can my life continue to fund itself when I am not actively working it?" That question changes everything. Because when the answer is yes, travel becomes easy. Motherhood becomes less financially threatening. Grief becomes survivable without financial panic layered on top of it. Relationships become less financially tense because dependence has become a choice rather than a requirement.

Real wealth is not the ability to buy a flight. It is the ability to take it without asking permission from your income.

Soft life is not movement. It is freedom from financial interruption when life requires you to pause.

The goal is not to work less. The goal is to build a life that does not punish you for resting.

Location freedom

There is a question underneath the time freedom conversation that does not always get asked directly.

Can you live where you genuinely want to live?

Not where the job requires you to be. Not where the rent is low enough to make the numbers work. Not where you ended up because of someone else's decision or someone else's opportunity. Where you actually want to be.

For some women that means staying in the city they love but finally being able to afford a neighborhood that feels right. For others, it means leaving an expensive city entirely once their income is no longer tied to a specific office building. For others it means splitting time between two places, spending winters somewhere warm and summers closer to family, or maintaining a base in the US while spending extended periods abroad. For many women it simply means moving closer to aging parents without the financial panic that would have made that decision impossible five years earlier.

Location freedom is one of the quietest forms of wealth because it rarely shows up in anyone's financial plan until they realize they have been living somewhere out of financial obligation rather than genuine choice. When your income travels with you, your options open in ways that a salary tied to one office in one city never allows.

Luxury without self-destruction

Let's talk about the things that we want.

The beautiful apartment. The designer bag you have been looking at for two years. The vacation that is not a budget trip but a real one, the kind where you stay somewhere that feels luxurious and you order what you want from the menu without doing the math in your head first. The wellness investment. The wardrobe that makes you feel like the version of yourself you are working toward.

None of that is wrong. None of it is shallow. None of it needs to be apologized for.

The only question worth asking is whether those things come from a position of genuine financial stability or from debt and performance anxiety. Because a designer bag purchased after your investments are funded, your emergency fund is full, and your savings are on track is a completely different financial event than the same bag purchased on credit to maintain an image your income cannot currently support.

The first one is a reward. The second one is a trap wearing beautiful packaging.

Enjoy the things that bring you genuine pleasure. Build the financial foundation first. And when the luxury arrives on the back of real stability rather than borrowed money, it feels completely different. You wear it differently. You sit in that vacation differently. Because nothing is attached to it except the satisfaction of having built something real.

Career design

One of the quiet gifts of financial independence is that it expands the range of what is possible for your career without forcing you to choose survival over preference.

Some women want to reach the C-suite and they should be fully supported in building toward that. Some want to leave corporate life entirely and build something of their own. Some want the flexibility of consulting, working deeply with a few clients on their own schedule rather than being available to one employer all day every day. Some want to step back to part-time during certain seasons of life, whether that is early motherhood, a health challenge, or simply a season of creative work that does not fit inside a traditional job description. Some want to spend years at home with their children and return to work later on their own terms.

All of these are valid. None of them is a lesser version of success.

The financial work this book has been building toward is precisely what makes genuine career design possible. When your income is not entirely dependent on one employer, when your investments are working in the background, when your emergency fund is solid and your savings are consistent, the shape of your career becomes a choice rather than a constraint. You can afford to leave a role that is no longer right for you. You can afford to take a lower salary for work that genuinely excites you. You can afford to pause and return on your own timeline.

No single path defines success. The path that defines your success is the one you design deliberately, with your eyes open and your finances stable enough to give you real options.

Relationship freedom

Money gives women options. And options change everything.

Financial independence means you can choose your relationships rather than being trapped in them by necessity. It means you can leave a job that is disrespectful, a living situation that is unsafe, a dynamic that is costing you more than money. It means the people in your life are there because you genuinely want them there, not because you cannot afford the alternative.

It is worth being honest about something that does not come up often enough in personal finance conversations. Financial dependence does not just create practical constraints. It creates vulnerability to control.

In unhealthy relationships, especially ones where one person begins to feel a loss of power, control tactics tend to escalate precisely when the dependent person shows signs of wanting to leave. This can look like financial manipulation, where access to money or accounts is used as leverage. It can look like threats designed to create fear and compliance. It can look like isolation from the support systems that might help someone find a way out.

These dynamics are not about love. They are about power retention. And the more financially dependent someone is, the more effective those tactics become. Financial independence does not guarantee that no one will ever try to control you. But it removes the mechanism that makes control tactics work. When you have your own income, your own accounts, your own emergency fund, and your own ability to survive independently, a threat loses most of its leverage.

A lot of content about the soft life focuses on comfort. The beautiful apartment, the wellness routine, the aesthetic Saturday morning. But real softness is something much more foundational than aesthetics. Real softness includes psychological safety. It includes exit options. It includes the autonomy to make decisions about your own life without calculating whether you can afford the consequences. It includes dignity under pressure.

Without those things, softness is performative. You can look soft online while being emotionally trapped offline.

Financial security does not prevent betrayal. It does not prevent heartbreak or loss or the complicated reality of human relationships. But it reduces captivity. It allows a woman to say "I am leaving" without first calculating where she will sleep, how she will eat, and how she will survive next month. That space to think clearly, to act from choice rather than fear, is what financial independence buys in the moments that matter most.

Legacy

At some point the question shifts again.

It stops being about what you can afford and becomes about what you want to leave behind.

This book is called *Her Life, Her Money*, and there is a reason those two things appear together in the title. The money is never the end of the story. It is how a woman gets to write the rest of it on her own terms, and eventually, it is how she passes something forward to the people who come after her.

What should remain because you lived?

For some women, the answer is educated children who did not have to start from zero the way she did. For others it is paid-off property that passes down without debt attached to it. For others it is charitable giving that funds a cause she cared about long after she is gone. For others it is the stability of a family that never has to experience the financial panic she spent her twenties navigating. For others it is a business, or an investment portfolio, or simply the knowledge and financial habits she modeled for the next generation so they start further ahead than she did.

Legacy does not require a dynasty. It requires intention.

Every financial decision you make today is also a decision about what you are building toward and what you are leaving behind. The savings account, the investment portfolio, the property, the business, the will, the trust, the estate plan, none of these are just financial instruments. They are evidence of a woman who thought carefully about her life, built something real with it, and decided that what she created was worth protecting and worth passing on.

That is the soft life in its fullest form. Not just comfort in the present. But peace about the future.

The goal was never to look rich.

The goal was to build a life so well-designed that peace became your greatest luxury.

That is what designing your soft life actually means. Not the aesthetics. Not the image. Not the performance of ease for an audience that is watching from behind a screen.

It means building a life where your income does not stop when you need to pause. Where your relationships exist by choice rather than necessity. Where your career reflects your actual priorities rather than your fear of running out of money. Where the people who come after you start from a stronger foundation than you did.

It means having the financial structure that lets you be fully present for the moments that matter, the ordinary Tuesday afternoons with your children, the phone calls with aging parents that do not feel rushed, the creative projects that do not pay immediately but feed something essential, the rest that your body and mind genuinely need.

The money is the tool. The life is the point.

Design it deliberately. Build it honestly. Protect it fiercely.

And do not let anyone tell you that wanting a life that feels as good as it looks is too much to ask for.

There is a difference between looking soft online and living softly in real life.

A woman can post luxury vacations, designer purchases, and aesthetic morning routines while privately living under extreme pressure. Overworked. Financially stretched. Emotionally exhausted. Carrying most of the household and childcare responsibilities. Unable to rest because everything stops if she does.

That gap between the image and the reality is worth naming honestly and without judgment, because it is more common than anyone's highlight reel suggests.

Social media has taught us to associate softness with consumption. Designer bags. Luxury travel. Expensive brunches. Beautiful apartments staged for photographs. Pilates classes at boutique studios. The aesthetic of ease.

But real softness is not aesthetics. Real softness is having margin. Having rest. Having options. Having time. Having support. Having the financial breathing room to pause when life requires it without everything unraveling.

The difference between a woman who experiences chronic hustle and a woman who experiences actual softness is rarely income alone. It is the structure underneath the income, the systems, the assets, the support, the choices made before the pressure arrived.

Motherhood and the Soft Life

One of the most significant determinants of whether a woman experiences softness or survival mode is the timing and structure of motherhood, and it is a conversation that personal finance books never honestly address.

For some women, waiting longer to have children is not selfishness. It is strategy. They want time to establish their careers, build their savings, eliminate debt, choose the right partner, create income streams that do not require their constant presence, and purchase property before adding the financial and emotional weight of raising children. They understand that motherhood without support, financial, practical, and emotional, can transform what was supposed to be a soft life into the hardest season they have ever navigated.

The cost of hustling through new motherhood is real and it is rarely discussed in the spaces where financial planning conversations happen. A woman recovering from childbirth while answering work emails is not living softly. A woman returning to work earlier than she is physically ready because the bills did not pause for her recovery is not living softly. A woman breastfeeding during meetings and managing school logistics at midnight while maintaining a polished professional presence is not soft. She is performing under pressure and calling it ambition.

More women are beginning to ask a question that the previous generation was rarely permitted to ask openly: do I want children right now, or do I first want the infrastructure that allows me to mother well? That infrastructure looks different for every woman but tends to include things like a solid savings base, flexible or remote work, a partner who genuinely shares the labor, accessible childcare, passive income that does not vanish when she steps back, health insurance that does not depend on her staying in a job she wants to leave, and the emotional readiness that comes from having done enough of her own healing before taking on the responsibility of someone else's entire world.

Some women will choose not to have children at all, and that is also part of modern financial autonomy. Not every woman's rich life includes motherhood. Some women's richest lives are built around travel, entrepreneurship, philanthropy, creative work, freedom of movement, and the peace that comes from a life designed entirely around their own priorities. That choice deserves to be named without the weight of social expectation attached to it.

A rich life is designed intentionally. Not copied socially.

There is an interesting parallel between what this book teaches about delayed financial gratification and what some women are now applying to life planning more broadly. Traditional finance advice says save first, invest first, build first before you spend. Some women are applying similar logic to their larger life decisions: stabilize first, heal first, choose wisely first, build the foundation before adding the weight. Not because motherhood lacks value. But because unsupported motherhood in a modern economy where most households require two incomes to function creates a level of strain that no amount of love can fully absorb.

It is also worth saying, clearly and without qualification, that waiting does not guarantee an easier path. Money does not eliminate the emotional demands of parenting. It does not make the sleepless nights shorter or the worry quieter. But it does reduce the avoidable suffering. And there is a meaningful difference between being tired from parenting and parenting while financially panicked.

A soft life is not expensive aesthetics. It is having enough support that your life does not constantly feel like survival.

10

The Partner effect

"Let's toast to paid mortgages, lasting marriages…"

— TALIB KWELI

There is an ancient text that has been quoted at weddings, cross-stitched onto pillows, and held up as the gold standard for what a wife should be. Most people who reference it focus on the part about the virtuous woman, her character, her kindness, her devotion. But read it carefully and what you find is a portrait of a financially independent, economically active woman who builds wealth, manages assets, and makes investment decisions within a household that functions because both partners understand their roles.

The Proverbs 31 woman buys and sells property. She considers a field and purchases it. She runs productive enterprises involving vineyards, trade, and textiles. She creates multiple income streams. She manages the household's resources with intention and skill. She is not waiting for provision alone. She is actively participating in wealth creation.

But here is what often gets missed in conversations about this passage. Her productivity is not happening in isolation or in chaos. It is supported by structure. Her husband is described as respected among community leaders, trusted with public responsibility, and known for his standing. He is not threatened by her capability. Her competence enhances the household rather than competing with it. His role and hers are complementary. There is dignity in both contributions.

The modern interpretation of that partnership is straightforward. A healthy partner does not shrink when you grow financially. He does not become insecure when your income rises, when your business succeeds, or when your name starts carrying weight in rooms he does not enter. Instead, he stabilizes the environment in which you grow, and that stability is one of the most underrated forms of support a partner can offer.

Many modern relationships fail financially not because of a lack of money, but because of what happens around money. Comparison. Resentment. Imbalance that goes unaddressed. Ego conflicts about who earns more or who contributes more. The Proverbs 31 model suggests a different framework entirely. Shared vision. Mutual respect. Defined responsibilities. Trust in each other's domains. The question stops being "who earns more?" and becomes "are we building in the same direction?"

Her productivity is also possible because the household is stable. She is not constantly operating in crisis mode. She has the mental and emotional space to plan ahead, to think long term, to take calculated risks, to pursue opportunities. That matters financially because instability destroys investment thinking, long-term planning, creativity, and business growth. A woman whose home life is chaotic, contentious, or emotionally draining does not have the same capacity for wealth building as a woman whose home is a foundation rather than a source of friction.

The Proverbs 31 woman is not a solo success story. She is a builder within a stable partnership, a decision-maker within a structured household, a wealth creator within a system that allows long-term thinking. Her finances flourish not because she is alone but because she is aligned.

That is the standard worth holding for any partnership you choose to build your life within.

It is also worth saying clearly what this chapter is not about. It is not about chasing wealth through a partner. Women who reduce their financial strategy to finding a rich man have outsourced their security to someone else's decisions, someone else's stability, and someone else's continued goodwill. That is not a financial plan. That is a dependency. Real financial partnership is built between two people who are each building something, who understand money, who communicate honestly about it, and who choose to combine their resources and their efforts because doing so makes both of them stronger.

Dating Versus Marriage: What You Actually Need to Know

Dating happens during everyone's highlight reel.

Polished appearances. Exciting experiences. Strong earning years with few major responsibilities. Minimal crises. Everyone is at their most optimistic, their most charming, their most financially comfortable version of themselves. You see how a person behaves when things are going well, which is useful information but genuinely incomplete information.

Marriage reveals something different entirely.

Marriage shows you how a person responds to postpartum recovery, to infertility struggles, to layoffs, to grief, to sick parents, to business failure, to caregiving burdens, to relocation, and to economic downturns. These are not edge cases. These are the seasons that every long marriage will move through at some point. The question is not whether difficulty will arrive. The question is who will be sitting across from you when it does, and whether that person will face it with you or make it harder.

This is why choosing a life partner is one of the most significant financial decisions a woman will ever make. Not because a partner is a financial strategy, but because the person you build your life with will shape the conditions under which every other financial decision gets made.

When I went on short-term leave to give birth to my second son, I found myself facing a financial reality I hadn't fully anticipated.

At that point in my career, I was earning more than my husband. On paper, we were doing well. But pregnancy introduced a temporary shift in our household finances.

The state we lived in did not offer paid family leave. My employer only provided short-term disability coverage for childbirth, and because I had not been at the company long enough, I didn't qualify for full parental leave benefits.

What made that season even harder was what happened inside our marriage.

As my maternity leave continued, I began realizing something I had never fully confronted before:

Our household was heavily dependent on my income.

That realization frightened me.

Not because my husband wasn't working.

Not because he lacked ambition.

But because I could suddenly see how vulnerable our household had become if one income, particularly mine, was interrupted.

And motherhood interrupted mine.

For the first time, my husband felt that pressure too.

He realized that if I stepped away for longer than expected, if complications arose, or if my career slowed down temporarily, the financial weight on him would increase significantly.

That awareness changed the atmosphere in our home.

Stress entered ordinary conversations, small disagreements became larger arguments, conversations about bills felt heavier.

Both of us were exhausted.

Both of us felt pressure.

And neither of us fully knew how to articulate the fear underneath it.

That's when something dangerous can begin to happen in relationships:

Resentment quietly grows where preparation was absent.

A woman may resent feeling like she cannot safely pause to recover from childbirth.

A man may resent the sudden financial expectations placed on him.

Both people may begin grieving the version of life they assumed they had built.

And often the argument isn't really about money.

It's about fear.

Fear of instability.
Fear of failure.
Fear of letting your family down.

This is why choosing a life partner matters so deeply.

You need someone who can face temporary seasons of imbalance without weaponizing those seasons later.

Because marriage will not always be 50/50. Sometimes it is 80/20. Sometimes it is 20/80.

Sometimes one person is physically recovering. Sometimes one person is grieving.

Sometimes one person is building a business. Sometimes one person loses a parent.

Sometimes one person must temporarily carry more.

Healthy couples understand that temporary imbalance is not permanent failure.

And that season taught me one of the greatest financial lessons of my life:

Do not just build wealth. Build a household that can survive interruptions to wealth.

That means emergency savings, adequate insurance, multiple income streams, honest financial conversations and choosing a partner emotionally mature enough to endure difficult seasons with you.

Because love is easy when both direct deposits hit on time.

Character is revealed when life interrupts the plan.

My income dropped during a season when our expenses were increasing.

We were preparing for a new baby while navigating reduced earnings.

That experience taught me something important:

A woman can be highly educated.
A woman can be career-driven.
A woman can be financially responsible.

And still encounter seasons where life requires her to lean on partnership.

This is why choosing a spouse based solely on current income, flashy displays of wealth, or lifestyle aesthetics is shortsighted.

The real question is:

Can this person help keep your household steady when life temporarily shifts your earning power?

Pregnancy complications, Career transitions, Family illness, Grief. Business setbacks.

These moments test the strength of a partnership.

In my case, I needed someone who understood that my reduced earnings were temporary, not a permanent reflection of my ambition or capabilities.

I needed a partner who could carry additional weight without resentment.

And that experience reinforced a lesson I want every woman to understand:

Do not simply choose someone who can afford your best moments. Choose someone who can help protect your hardest ones.

The real question isn't:

"Can this person fund vacations?"

It's:

"Can this person remain steady when life becomes expensive emotionally, physically, and financially?"

The Role of a Partner's Income in Building Wealth

One of the most practical ways to understand what financial partnership creates is to look at what a second income makes possible beyond simply covering more expenses.

The chart below shows the relative ways a partner's income contributes to wealth building. It is important to read it correctly. This is not a chart about where money gets spent. It is a chart about what becomes financially possible when two incomes are working together strategically rather than just covering the cost of a shared life.

Role of a Partner's Income in Building Wealth

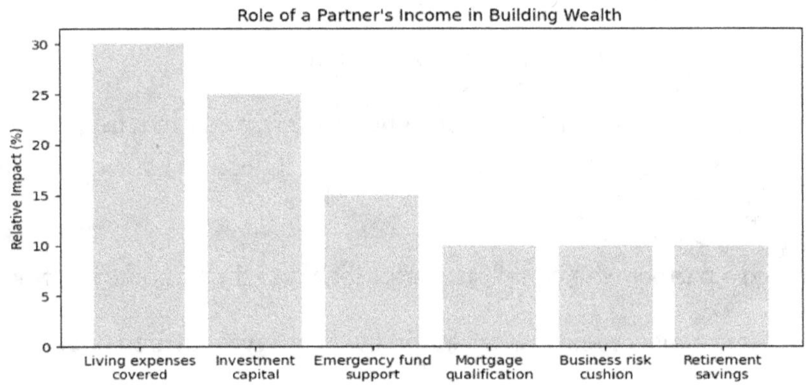

The chart shows the relative ways a partner's income supports wealth creation, not necessarily how money is spent.

Each category represents a structural advantage that becomes available when two incomes work together inside a coordinated financial system.

1. Living Expenses Covered (30%) – Largest Impact

This is the tallest bar because a second income often pays for housing, food, utilities, childcare, and daily expenses.

When one income covers necessities, the other income can be invested rather than consumed. This creates more capital for wealth-building.

2. Investment Capital (25%)

Once basic needs are covered, additional income can be redirected into assets that grow over time.

This includes investments such as index funds, equities, real estate deposits, retirement contributions, and business ventures.

This is the second-largest contributor because invested money can compound over time.

3. Emergency Fund Support (15%)

Having two incomes makes it easier to build cash reserves.

Cash reserves act as protection against life's unpredictability. They prevent situations in which investments must be sold prematurely or debt must be taken on under pressure.

An emergency fund does not create wealth directly, but it protects it.

4. Mortgage Qualification (10%)

Lenders often consider household income.

A second income can increase borrowing power and help purchase appreciating assets such as property.

This matter because access to credit, when used wisely, can accelerate asset ownership rather than delay it.

5. Business Risk Cushion (10%)

If one partner starts a business, studies, changes careers, or invests aggressively, the other's income can help stabilize household finances. This flexibility can create opportunities for higher future returns.

6. Retirement Savings (10%)

Additional income can increase contributions to pensions, retirement accounts, and long-term investments.

Even modest contributions can become significant through compounding.

When viewed this way, partnership is not simply emotional or logistical.

It becomes structural.

Grief can temporarily destabilize finances

This is one of the most important things nobody tells you during the early stages of a relationship, when everything is exciting and the future feels like it belongs entirely to you and the person sitting across from you.

Grief is expensive. Not just emotionally. Financially.

When a parent becomes ill, you may find yourself contributing to hospital bills you did not plan for. You may need emergency travel at short notice. You may inherit family responsibilities that consume time you were previously using to earn. Your productivity drops. Your emotional capacity shrinks. You may need to pause work temporarily, and the financial system does not pause with you.

After losing a parent the costs continue. Funeral expenses. Legal paperwork. Estate administration. In many cases supporting a surviving parent or other family members who relied on the person you just lost. These obligations are real, they arrive without warning, and they arrive at the moment when you have the least emotional capacity to manage them.

In many families across the US and globally, these obligations extend beyond the immediate household and become a significant financial responsibility for the children of the family, often the most financially stable child, and very often a daughter.

A healthy partner responds to difficult seasons with a simple message: "We'll figure this out together." When my mother passed away in my early thirties, my husband did exactly that. His unwavering support became an anchor during one of the most painful periods of my life, and for that, I will always be grateful.

An unhealthy partner, however, often responds very differently- with resentment, emotional withdrawal, or financial pressure that compounds the grief instead of helping to carry it.

The difference between these two responses is profound. One deepens trust, strengthens the relationship, and reminds you that you are not facing life's challenges alone. The other creates distance at the very moment when partnership is needed most.

Setbacks reveal financial maturity

Anyone can look generous, patient, and emotionally stable during abundance.

The real information about a person's financial character does not arrive during the good seasons. It arrives during the difficult ones. And the difficult ones will come for everyone without exception.

Observe their behavior during times of unemployment. Not the first week when the shock is fresh and the severance is still in the account. Observe the third month, when the savings are thinning and the rejection emails are piling up and the pressure is becoming genuinely difficult to carry. Do they panic and make reckless financial decisions? Do they blame everyone around them for circumstances that are partly or entirely within their control? Do they quit at the first sign of real difficulty and pivot to the next idea before giving anything a genuine chance to work?

Watch closely how they respond to a failed business. Not the polished LinkedIn post about lessons learned. Watch even closer what happens inside the household during the months when the business is failing and the decision to close it has not yet been made. Do they hide the financial reality from you? Do they become defensive when you ask honest questions about where things stand? Do they make unilateral decisions about shared finances without discussion?

Study how they handle a career pivot, a medical emergency, a family crisis, a moment of public embarrassment, or any situation where the version of themselves they have been presenting to the world is suddenly under pressure.

Do they communicate honestly with you about what is happening?

Do they problem solve steadily and methodically rather than reacting emotionally to every new development?

Do they remain ethical under pressure, honoring their financial commitments even when it is difficult?

Do they rebuild patiently, understanding that recovery is a process rather than an event?

These are not abstract character questions. They are financial questions. Because the person who panics, blames, hides, and quits during their own setbacks will bring those same responses to the shared financial life of your household when difficulty arrives there too.

You will learn more about a potential partner's true financial character from one difficult season than from years of smooth sailing together.

Pay attention accordingly.

A flashy person who displays immense amounts of wealth may have debt, poor discipline, family money they didn't build or unsustainable spending habits.

Meanwhile someone less flashy may be investing consistently, building a business, increasing skills, showing discipline and planning long term.

Before visible success often comes long periods of ordinary discipline.

When evaluating a potential partner, it is important to look beyond appearances and pay attention to the financial habits and values that shape their everyday life. As women, we often discuss amongst each other the checks we should make before moving forward in a relationship. "Green" flags are signs that suggest a healthy foundation, while red flags signal areas that deserve caution and closer attention.

Green flags that actually matter

Beyond income and appearance, there are deeper indicators of long-term compatibility and stability.

Emotional steadiness is one. The ability to remain grounded during uncertainty matters far more than charisma during comfort.

Work ethic and consistency are another. Not intensity in bursts, but the ability to show up reliably over time.

Financial honesty is essential. Transparency about money, even when imperfect, builds trust that supports long-term planning.

Problem-solving ability is also critical. Life will not always present neat solutions. The ability to think clearly under pressure is a protective asset in any partnership.

Equally important is ambition paired with realism. Drive without grounding can create instability. But direction combined with awareness creates sustainable progress.

Finally, generosity matters when it is balanced. Giving without recklessness reflects both compassion and discipline.

And perhaps most importantly, there is respect for your own growth. A partner who supports your evolution rather than competing with it strengthens the foundation of the relationship.

Red flags

There are also patterns that should not be ignored.

Performative luxury, especially when it is disconnected from actual financial structure, can signal instability.

Financial secrecy often indicates lack of transparency, which can become a long-term issue in shared planning.

Entitlement without contribution creates imbalance that becomes more difficult over time.

A refusal to plan for the future is not simplicity. It is avoidance.

Mocking your ambition or downplaying your goals can signal insecurity rather than partnership.

Irresponsibility toward family obligations may reflect deeper patterns of inconsistency.

And a repeated pattern of quitting during difficulty often points to limited resilience under pressure.

These traits matter not because people are perfect, but because long-term partnership requires adaptability, accountability, and shared responsibility.

The goal is not to find someone who is rich. The goal is to find someone whose financial habits, values, and decision making will support the life you hope to build together.

Motherhood, Caregiving, and Career Tradeoffs

There is a conversation that happens in women's minds long before it ever gets spoken out loud, sometimes long before there is even a partner in the picture to have it with.

What happens to my career when I have children?

Not what should happen. Not what the company handbook says about parental leave. But what happens, in practice, to a woman's earning trajectory, her professional momentum, her retirement contributions, and her long-term financial independence when she takes on the responsibilities of motherhood in a world that was largely not designed with her in mind.

The research on this is consistent and sobering. Economists call it the child penalty, the measurable drop in a woman's earnings and career advancement that tends to follow the birth of a child, a drop that does not occur in the same way or to the same degree for men. Women are more likely to reduce their working hours after having children. They are more likely to leave the workforce temporarily or permanently. They are more likely to turn down promotions, travel, and high-visibility opportunities because the invisible labor of running a household and raising children falls disproportionately on them. And the financial consequences of those decisions compound over time through lower lifetime earnings, smaller retirement balances, reduced Social Security benefits, and diminished long-term wealth.

None of this is said to discourage motherhood. It is said to make the financial reality visible so that it can be planned for honestly rather than discovered in the middle of a maternity leave with a mortgage payment due.

The career tradeoffs of motherhood are real. The question is how to navigate them with your financial independence as intact as possible, and that navigation begins long before the first child arrives.

It begins with the partner you choose. A partner who genuinely shares the domestic labor, who takes parental leave when it is available, who does the school pickup and the pediatrician appointments and the sick day coverage, is not just being a good parent. He is protecting your earning power. Every hour of domestic labor he carries is an hour you can direct toward your career, your business, your investments, or simply your own rest and recovery.

It begins with the financial foundation you build before children arrive. Emergency funds that can absorb a period of reduced income. Multiple income streams that do not all depend on your full-time presence. Retirement contributions that are already established and can continue even at reduced levels. An investment portfolio that is already working in the background. These are not luxuries. They are the infrastructure that makes it possible to step back without stepping off the financial map entirely.

It begins with honest conversations about what motherhood will actually look like in your specific household, not the idealized version, but the real one. Who will handle childcare when a child is sick and both parents have important commitments? Who adjusts their schedule when school starts earlier than expected? Who manages the mental load of tracking pediatric appointments, school events, dietary restrictions, and the thousand small logistics that keeping children healthy and thriving requires? These conversations are financial conversations even when they do not feel like it, because the answers determine whose career gets prioritized and whose financial growth gets temporarily or permanently constrained.

Caregiving extends beyond children too. At some point many women find themselves in what researchers call the sandwich generation, caught between raising children and caring for aging parents simultaneously. The financial cost of that season is significant and rarely planned for. Time taken away from work for caregiving. Money contributed to a parent's medical care or housing. Emotional and physical energy that would otherwise be directed toward career growth or wealth building. These are real costs that fall disproportionately on women and that deserve a place in any honest financial plan.

The women who navigate these seasons with their financial independence most intact tend to share certain characteristics. They built financial resilience before they needed it. They chose partners who shared the load genuinely rather than performatively. They maintained their own financial identity throughout marriage, their own accounts, their own credit history, their own professional development. And they made the tradeoffs they made consciously, with clear eyes about what they were choosing and what it would cost, rather than simply absorbing whatever the circumstances demanded of them.

The career tradeoffs of motherhood and caregiving are not avoidable. But they are navigable. And the degree to which they permanently alter your financial trajectory depends enormously on the preparation, the partnership, and the financial infrastructure you have in place when they arrive.

Divorce, Breakups, and Starting Over Financially

Nobody gets into a serious relationship planning for it to end and this book would not be complete without an honest conversation about what happens when it does.

Divorce in the United States is common. According to data from the American Psychological Association, roughly forty to fifty percent of marriages end in divorce. Second marriages end at even higher rates. And the financial consequences of divorce fall disproportionately on women, particularly women who reduced their working hours during the marriage, who took career interruptions for childrearing, or who allowed their financial identity to become too merged with a partner's to the point where untangling it becomes genuinely complicated.

The financial cost of divorce is not just the legal fees, though those can be substantial. It is the division of assets that were built together. It is the loss of a second income that was covering half the mortgage. It is the potential need to reenter the workforce at a disadvantaged position after years away. It is the retirement savings that get split in half at exactly the moment when compounding most needs time to work. It is the credit history that was tied to a joint account. It is the home that needs to be sold or refinanced. It is the children whose needs do not stop because the marriage did.

This is not a reason to avoid commitment. It is a reason to protect yourself financially within it.

The women who recover most successfully from the financial disruption of divorce tend to have done certain things during the marriage that most people do not think to do until after the marriage ends. They maintained their own financial identity throughout. Their own bank accounts. Their own credit cards in their own name. Their own credit history. Their own professional development and earning capacity. They stayed connected to their own finances rather than delegating that responsibility entirely to a partner. They knew what the household owned, what it owed, and what the plan was. They were a participant in the financial life of the marriage, not a passenger.

If you are currently in a relationship where you have drifted away from your own financial independence, it is not too late to reestablish it. Open an account in your own name. Rebuild your own credit profile if it has lapsed. Stay engaged with your own professional development.

Understand the household finances well enough that nothing would be a complete surprise if circumstances changed.

This is not cynicism about love. This is wisdom about life.

Breakups outside of marriage carry their own financial complications, particularly when couples have shared expenses, joint leases, combined investments, or intertwined finances without the legal framework that marriage provides. The absence of legal protection in an unmarried partnership means that untangling shared finances often depends entirely on goodwill and honesty from both parties, which is available in abundance when the relationship is good and can disappear entirely when it ends.

Starting over financially after a significant relationship ends is genuinely hard. It requires rebuilding a budget around one income instead of two. It may require moving, changing childcare arrangements, adjusting retirement contributions, rebuilding savings that were depleted by the transition, and doing all of this while managing the emotional weight of a major life change.

But it is survivable. And for many women, the financial rebuilding that follows the end of a relationship becomes the moment they finally build a financial life that is entirely their own, on their own terms, without compromise or negotiation. There is something powerful about that, even when it arrives wrapped in difficulty.

The most important thing to understand about financial recovery after a relationship ends is that it is a process, not an event. It does not happen all at once. It happens one decision at a time, one month at a time, one rebuilt account and one renewed investment contribution and one reclaimed financial habit at a time. And the women who have done it consistently say the same thing: it was hard, and it was worth it, and they wish they had started protecting their financial independence earlier.

Afterword

"Look way deep inside yourself/Discover the diamond inside, find your wealth once you get it, you gotta live it to the limit"

— NAS

One of the biggest lessons I've learned on my journey toward financial freedom is that rigid people often miss life-changing opportunities because they are too attached to one path.

When I was younger, I thought wealth had to be built in a very specific way. I believed there was one respectable career path, one type of investment I should focus on, and one timeline I had to follow. But real life quickly taught me that financial freedom often requires flexibility, and sometimes that flexibility looks nothing like what you imagined when you first set out.

I know this from personal experience in a way that still makes me smile when I think about it.

Early in my career, I briefly took on a role as an executive assistant simply to get my foot in the door at a company I genuinely wanted to work for. My days were spent organizing travel, scheduling meetings, and occasionally picking up lunch for executives who were doing the exact kind of work I was working toward. On paper, the role had nothing to do with where I was headed. It was not aligned with my long-term career goals. It was not what I had studied for or what I had imagined for myself when I was completing my MBA.

But it served an important purpose that I could not have understood fully until I was on the other side of it.

It gave me access to opportunities I might not have had otherwise. It put me in rooms I would not have entered through the front door. It showed me up close how decisions were made, how money moved, and how the people I wanted to learn from actually operated when no one was performing for an audience. And perhaps most valuably, it reinforced with complete clarity what I did and did not want for my future.

Sometimes the jobs we take are not stepping stones toward our dream career. They are lessons that provide the kind of clarity that no classroom and no career counselor can give you. That experience reminded me that I wanted a different path, and that realization was just as valuable as any promotion or professional achievement I have ever had.

Remaining flexible does not mean abandoning your goals. It means being willing to take unexpected opportunities, learn from them honestly, and use the insights you gain to move closer to the life and career you truly want. The path is rarely straight. The people who build the most meaningful financial lives are almost never the ones who followed the exact plan they set at 22. They are the ones who stayed clear about where they were going while remaining genuinely open about how they would get there.

There were other moments of flexibility too. Moments where I had to be willing to explore unfamiliar opportunities because they offered higher earning potential even when they felt like detours. Moments where a position gave me not a better salary but something equally valuable, more freedom over my time and more space to think strategically about where I was building toward. Each of those pivots created room for me to earn more, save more, and eventually design the kind of life this book has been describing from the very first chapter.

I also learned that flexibility matters just as much in investing as it does in careers. There are seasons where one asset class performs better than another. At one point real estate may be your strongest wealth-building tool. In another season equities, business ownership, or even cash preservation may be the wiser move. Wealth builders who refuse to evolve often stay attached to underperforming strategies simply because change feels uncomfortable and familiarity feels safe.

The world also changes quickly. Entire industries get disrupted by technology. New business models emerge seemingly overnight. Digital platforms create income opportunities that did not exist a decade ago. The people who stay genuinely open-minded are almost always the first to benefit from those shifts, not because they chased every trend, but because they were paying attention and willing to move when the moment called for it.

Remaining flexible does not mean chasing every trend or abandoning the long-term discipline this book has been built on. It means being wise enough to recognize when a pivot is necessary and honest enough with yourself to make it before circumstances force your hand.

Sometimes financial growth looks like changing industries. Sometimes it looks like learning a new skill that was not on your original plan. Sometimes it looks like leaving behind an investment strategy that served you in one season but no longer fits where you are going. And sometimes it simply means admitting there may be a better way to build wealth than the one you originally imagined.

Your financial goals may stay the same. Your methods may need to evolve.

Remain grounded in your values, but flexible in your approach.

Because financial freedom rarely belongs to the person who had the perfect plan from day one.

It often belongs to the person who was willing to adapt.

Financial freedom requires long-term thinking. But long-term thinking also requires accepting that the world will not stay the same, and perhaps no force is reshaping the world more rapidly right now than artificial intelligence.

Technology is already changing how people work, earn, invest, and build businesses in ways that would have seemed extraordinary even five years ago. Artificial intelligence is one of the biggest shifts of our generation, and its impact will likely reshape entire industries in ways we are only beginning to understand.

Jobs that once felt completely secure are becoming automated. Administrative tasks, customer service roles, basic design work, data entry, and repetitive knowledge work are already being transformed by tools like OpenAI's ChatGPT, Google's Gemini, and Microsoft's Copilot. Entire companies are learning how to accomplish more with significantly fewer people, and that trend is not slowing down.

At the same time, artificial intelligence is creating genuine new opportunities for people who are willing to engage with it rather than resist it. Entrepreneurs can now automate customer service, marketing content, business operations, and research at a fraction of the cost those functions required just a few years ago. Small business owners can scale faster with leaner teams. Creators can build and distribute digital products faster than ever before. Professionals who develop fluency with AI tools are becoming measurably more productive and more valuable in the workplace, which translates directly into stronger negotiating positions and higher earning potential.

The lesson is not to fear technology. It is to remain genuinely aware of how quickly industries can shift and to position yourself on the right side of that shift before it becomes obvious to everyone else.

If your entire financial future depends on one job, one skill set, one industry, or one business model that is already showing signs of disruption, the time to adapt is before the disruption fully arrives, not after.

The questions worth asking continuously are these. What skills are becoming more valuable as the economy evolves? What industries are growing rather than contracting? What tasks can technology now replace, and how does that change what your time and expertise are worth? How can you use new tools to increase your earning power rather than having those tools used to replace you? Where is consumer behavior shifting, and what does that create in terms of new needs and new opportunities?

Financial freedom belongs to people who can evolve with the times. This may mean learning to use AI tools that make you significantly more productive. It may mean investing in industries that are positioned to benefit from technological growth. It may mean building businesses designed to solve the problems of the future rather than the problems of the past.

Your goal is not to predict every change perfectly. Nobody can do that.

Your goal is to remain adaptable enough that when the world changes, you can change with it.

Because wealth is not just built through hard work alone.

In many seasons, it is built by those who recognize change early and position themselves accordingly.

Personal Closing from Author to Reader

A Final Word

When I started writing this book, I thought about the younger version of myself sitting in my apartment, staring at a budget spreadsheet at midnight, trying to figure out how someone could work this hard and still feel so much financial uncertainty.

Nobody had given her a clear map. Nobody had sat her down and explained how compounding worked, or what a vesting schedule meant, or why the partner she chose would shape her financial trajectory as much as any investment she ever made. She was figuring it out alone, one expensive lesson at a time, in a city that had no patience for learning curves.

This book is the conversation I wish someone had sat down and had with me back then.

Not a lecture. Not a list of rules. A real conversation between two women who understand that money is not just numbers on a page. It is freedom. It is options. It is the ability to leave what does not serve you and build what does. It is the difference between surviving your life and actually designing it.

Everything in the pages of this book all point toward the same thing.

A life that belongs to you.

Not to your employer. Not to your debt. Not to someone else's expectations of what a woman should want or how much space she should take up or how ambitious she is allowed to be.

To you.

You do not have to have it all figured out right now. You do not have to start with a large income or a perfect credit score or a clear five-year plan. You just have to start. One decision at a time. One account opened, one contribution made, one conversation had, one boundary drawn, one opportunity taken even when it looks nothing like what you imagined.

Allowing someone to dictate your finances hands them the power to dictate your life.

Build your financial life on a foundation that belongs to you. Protect it deliberately. Grow it patiently. And never let anyone convince you that wanting genuine freedom, the kind that does not depend on anyone's continued goodwill or approval, is too much to ask for.

It is not too much.

It is exactly enough.

Thank you for reading. Now go build something.

Christina

www.ingramcontent.com/pod-product-compliance
Lightning Source LLC
LaVergne TN
LVHW022223200926
848481LV00006B/2100
* 9 7 9 8 2 3 4 1 1 1 2 7 2 *